The Silver Series of Classics

ALFRED TENNYSON.

TENNYSON'S

THE PRINCESS: A MEDLEY

EDITED WITH INTRODUCTION AND NOTES

BY

JAMES CHALMERS, Ph.D., LL.D.

FELLOW OF THE UNIVERSITY OF ST. ANDREWS, SCOTLAND

SILVER, BURDETT AND COMPANY

New York   BOSTON   Chicago

PUBLISHERS' ANNOUNCEMENT.

THE SILVER SERIES OF ENGLISH CLASSICS is designed to furnish editions of many of the standard classics in English and American literature, in the best possible form for reading and study. While planned to meet the requirements for entrance examinations to college, as formulated by the Commission of American Colleges, it serves a no less important purpose in providing valuable and attractive reading for the use of the higher grades of public and private schools.

It is now generally recognized that to familiarize students with the masterpieces of literature is the best means of developing true literary taste, and of establishing a love of good reading which will be a permanent delight. The habit of cultured original expression is also established through the influence of such study.

To these ends, carefully edited and annotated editions of the Classics, which shall direct pupils in making intelligent and appreciative study of each work as a whole, and, specifically, of its individual features, are essential in the classroom.

The SILVER SERIES notably meets this need, through the editing of its volumes by scholars of high literary ability and educational experience. It unfolds the treasures of literary art, and shows the power and beauty of our language in the various forms of English composition, — as the oration, the essay, the argument, the biography, the poem, etc.

Thus, the first volume contains Webster's oration at the laying of the corner stone of Bunker Hill monument ; and, after a brief sketch of the orator's life, the *oration* is defined, — the speech itself furnishing a practical example of what a masterpiece in oratory should be.

Next follows the *essay*, as exemplified by Macaulay's " Essay on Milton." The story of the life of the great essayist creates an interest in his work, and the student, before he proceeds to study the essay, is shown in the Introduction the difference between the oratorical and the essayistic style.

3

775

After this, Burke's "Speech on Conciliation" is treated in a similar manner, the essential principles of *forensic* authorship being set forth.

Again, De Quincey's "Flight of a Tartar Tribe" — a conspicuous example of pure *narration* — exhibits the character and quality of this department of literary composition.

Southey's "Life of Nelson" is presented in the same personal and critical manner, placing before the student the essential characteristics of the *biographical* style.

The series continues with specimens of such works as : "The Rime of the Ancient Mariner," by Coleridge ; the "Essay on Burns," by Carlyle ; the "Sir Roger de Coverley Papers," by Addison ; Milton's "Paradise Lost," Books I. and II. ; Pope's "Iliad," Books I., VI., XXII., and XXIV. ; Dryden's "Palamon and Arcite" ; Shakespeare's "Merchant of Venice" ; Spenser's "Faerie Queene" ; Scott's "Lay of the Last Minstrel" ; Shelley's "Prometheus," and other works of equally eminent writers, covering a large and diversfied area of literary exposition.

The beginner, as well as the somewhat advanced scholar, will find in this series ample instruction and guidance for his own study, without being perplexed by abstruse or doubtful problems.

With the same thoughtfulness for the student's progress, the appended Notes provide considerable information outright ; but they are also designed to stimulate the student in making researches for himself, as well as in applying, under the direction of the teacher, the principles laid down in the critical examination of the separate divisions.

A portrait, either of the author or of the personage about whom he writes, will form an attractive feature of each volume. The text is from approved editions, keeping as far as possible the original form ; and the contents offer, at a very reasonable price, the latest results of critical instruction in the art of literary expression.

The teacher will appreciate the fact that enough, and not too much, assistance is rendered the student, leaving the instructor ample room for applying and extending the principles and suggestions which have been presented.

INTRODUCTION.

ALFRED TENNYSON was born on August 6, 1809, at Somersby, a small village in Lincolnshire, England. His father, who was rector of the parish, was notable for his scholarly and artistic tastes; his mother, for her sweetness of character and powers of imagination. Both parents had great influence over Tennyson in forming his character. Of the children, several were gifted with the imaginative temperament. Two sons older than Alfred became known as poets.

Charles, one year older than Alfred, was his favorite brother and constant companion. It was Charles with whom he studied, and talked, and wrote, and rambled over the beautiful valleys of famous Lincolnshire. The two boys began to write verse almost as soon as they could write anything. In fact, the whole family of boys at the rectory are roughly described by a contemporary neighbor as "running about from one place to another, known to everybody, and with ways of their own; they all wrote verses, they never had any pocket-money, they took long walks at night-time, and they were decidedly exclusive."

Charles and Alfred Tennyson, while yet youths, published, in 1827, a small volume of poetry entitled "Poems by Two Brothers." The following year the two brothers entered Trinity College, Cambridge, where Alfred gained the University Chancellor's gold medal for a poem on "Timbuctoo," and where he formed an intimate friendship with Arthur Henry Hallam, whose memory he has immortalized in "In Memoriam." Among his other intimate friends at Cambridge, who afterwards became famous, may be mentioned Henry Alford, Charles Merivale, James Spedding, F. D. Maurice, C. S. Venables, R. M. Milnes, R. C. Trench, J. M. Kemble, W. H. Brookfield, and Edmund and Henry Lushington, to the latter of whom he dedicated "The Princess." The most important of Tennyson's intimates at the university were Richard Monckton Milnes (afterwards Lord Houghton) and Arthur Henry Hallam, who was to become the poet's closest friend. Both of these companions were unsuccessful competitors with Tennyson for the Chancellor's prize in poetry in 1829.

In 1830 Tennyson published his "Poems, Chiefly Lyrical," which gave him at once a national standing, and, with some adverse notes, won him much praise, even from critics like Coleridge. In the same year his brother Charles published a volume of poems, which was also well received by the public. Wordsworth, among others, even held Charles to be the better poet of the two. In 1831, owing to his father's death, Tennyson left Cambridge without taking a degree.

The following year he published another volume entitled "Poems," which showed, in depth of thought, keenness of insight, and genuine dramatic power, a very great advance over the former volume. These two early volumes, although generally well received and heartily appreciated by the public, met with enough hostile criticism to put an end to his publishing for some years. Tennyson, who was naturally shy and retiring, and who had formed a habit of reserve that continued through life, was always very sensitive to adverse criticism, and he himself said, "The Reviews stopped me." For fully ten years he remained silent.

In 1842 came the publication of the "Poems by Alfred Tennyson," in two volumes — the first being mainly a reprint of the poems published ten years earlier, while the second was almost entirely new. From this dates his fame. There was now no lack of appreciation from any quarter. Even the very Reviews, which had so severely criticised him ten years earlier, now had only terms of the highest praise. Words of heartiest appreciation came from America and from all parts of the world. Henceforth he was to be the most widely popular of poets. Of all modern English poets, Tennyson has the most readers.

With the publication of the "Poems" in 1842, his reputation as a poet was permanently established, though his greatest works were yet to come. Chief among these are "The Princess" (1847), "In Memoriam" (1850), "Maud" (1855), "Idylls of the King" (1859–1885), and "Enoch Arden" (1864).

Of the three kinds of poetry — lyric, epic, and dramatic — Tennyson had now been eminently successful in the first, and moderately successful in the second; it remained for him to attempt the third and highest. Accordingly, in 1875, Tennyson published his first drama, "Queen Mary," followed by "Harold" (1877), "The Cup" (1881), "The

Promise of May" (1882), "The Falcon," and "Becket" (1884). On the death of Wordsworth, in 1850, Tennyson had been appointed Poet Laureate. In 1884 he was created a peer, with the title Baron Tennyson of D'Eyncourt. Until 1850 Tennyson had lived mainly in or near London; marrying that year, he settled at Twickenham, but soon moved to Aldworth in Surrey. Much of his later years, Tennyson spent with his family in their pleasant home at Farringford, Isle of Wight. He died at Aldworth House on October 6, 1892.

TENNYSON'S HOME, FARRINGFORD.

BIOGRAPHICAL AND BIBLIOGRAPHICAL OUTLINE.

1809. Born at Somersby, Lincolnshire, England.
1814–20. At Cadney's Village School and Louth Grammar-School.

1827. Publication of "Poems by Two Brothers."

1828. Entered Trinity College, Cambridge.

1829. Won the Chancellor's Prize Poem, "Timbuctoo."

1830. Published "Poems, Chiefly Lyrical."

1831. Death of his father; quits the university.

1832. Publishes "Poems by Alfred Tennyson."

1833. Death of Arthur Henry Hallam.

1842. Published "Poems by Alfred Tennyson," in two volumes.

1845. Pension of £200 granted by the government.

1847. Published "The Princess."

1850. Published "In Memoriam"; appointed Poet Laureate; married.

1852. "Ode on the Death of the Duke of Wellington."

1853. Settled at Farringford, Isle of Wight.

1854. "Charge of the Light Brigade."

1855. "Maud and Other Poems"; degree of D.C.L. from Oxford.

1857. "Enid and Nimuë: The True and the False."

1859. "Idylls of the King," in four parts.

1860. "Sea Dreams."

1861. "The Sailor Boy."

1864. "Enoch Arden."

1867. Purchased Aldworth Estate, Surrey.

1869. "The Holy Grail and Other Poems."

1871. "The Last Tournament."

1872. "Gareth and Lynette."

1875. "Queen Mary: A Drama."

1877. "Harold: A Drama."

1879. "Defense of Lucknow."

1880. "Ballads and Other Poems."

1881. "Despair"; "The Cup" (acted).

1882. "The Promise of May."

1884. "The Falcon"; "Becket." Created Baron of D'Eyncourt.

1886. "Locksley Hall Sixty Years After."

1888. Publication of collected edition of works, in eight volumes.

1889. "Idylls of the King," in twelve books.

1892. Died, October 6. Publication, October 28, of "Death of Œnone, Akbar's Dream, and Other Poems."

1894. First complete edition of Tennyson's works. Macmillan & Co.

SELECTED CRITICAL REFERENCES.

Bagehot's " Literary Studies."

Bayne's " Lessons from My Masters."

Brimley's " Essays."

Brooke's " Tennyson: His Art and Relation to Modern Life."

Church's " In the Laureate's Country."

Collins's " Illustrations of Tennyson."

Cooke's " Poets and Problems."

Dawson's " The Princess: A Study."

Dixon's " Primer of Tennyson."

Dowden's " Studies in Literature."

Gosse's " Early Victorian Literature."

Horne's " A New Spirit of the Age."

Hutton's " Literary Essays."

Jennings's " Lord Tennyson."

Kingsley's " Literary Essays."

Lowell's " Conversations with the Poets."

Napier's " Homes and Haunts of Alfred, Lord Tennyson."

Rolfe's " The Princess."

Saintsbury's " Nineteenth Century Literature."

Shepherd's " Tennysoniana."

Stedman's " Victorian Poets."

Tainsh's " A Study of the Works of Tennyson."

Tennyson's " Alfred, Lord Tennyson. A Memoir." By his Son (1897).

Tollemache's " Tennyson's Social Philosophy."

Van Dyke's " The Poetry of Tennyson."

APPRECIATIONS.

"In this work Mr. Tennyson shows himself more than ever the poet of the day. In it, more than ever, the old is interpenetrated with the new; the domestic and scientific, with the ideal and sentimental. He dares, in every page, to make use of modern words and notions, from which the mingled clumsiness and archaism of his compeers shrink, as unpoetical. Though his stage is an ideal fairyland, yet he has reached the ideal by the only true method — by bringing the Middle Age forward to the present one, and not by ignoring the present to fall back on a cold and galvanized mediævalism; and thus he makes the 'Medley' a mirror of the nineteenth century, possessed of its own new art and science, its own new temptations and aspirations, and yet grounded on and continually striving to reproduce the forms and experiences of all past time. The idea, too, of 'The Princess' is an essentially modern one. In every age women have been tempted, by the possession of superior beauty, intellect, or strength of will, to deny their own womanhood and attempt to stand alone as men, whether on the ground of political intrigue, ascetic saintship, or philosophic pride. Cleopatra and St. Hedwiga, Madame de Staël and the Princess, are merely different manifestations of the same self-willed and proud longing of woman to unsex herself, and realize, single and self-sustained, some distorted and partial notion of her own as to what the 'angelic life' should be. Cleopatra acted out the pagan ideal of an angel; St.

Hedwiga, the mediæval one; Madame de Staël, hers, with
the peculiar notions of her time as to what 'spiritual'
might mean; and in 'The Princess' Mr. Tennyson has
embodied the ideal of that nobler, wider, purer, yet equally
fallacious, because equally unnatural, analogue, which we
may now meet too often up and down England. He
shows us the woman, when she takes her stand on the
false, masculine ground of intellect, working out her own
moral punishment, by destroying in herself the tender
heart of flesh; not even her vast purposes of philan-
thropy can preserve her, for they are built up, not on the
womanhood which God has given her, but on her own
self-will; they change, they fall, they become inconsist-
ent, even as she does herself, till at last she loses all
feminine sensibility; scornfully and stupidly she rejects
and misunderstands the heart of man; and then, falling
from pride to sternness, from sternness to sheer inhu-
manity, she punishes sisterly love as a crime, robs the
mother of her child, and becomes all but a vengeful fury,
with all the peculiar faults of woman and none of the
peculiar excellences of man. . . . How Mr. Tennyson can
have attained the prodigal fullness of thought and imagery
which distinguishes this poem, and especially the last
canto, without his style ever becoming overloaded, seldom
even confused, is perhaps one of the greatest marvels of
the whole production. The songs themselves, which have
been inserted between the cantos in the last edition, seem,
perfect as they are, wasted and smothered among the sur-
rounding fertility, till we discover that they stand there,
not merely for the sake of their intrinsic beauty, but

serve to call the reader's mind, at every pause in the tale of the Princess's folly, to that very healthy ideal of womanhood which she has spurned.

"At the end of the first canto, fresh from the description of the female college, with its professoresses and hostleresses and other Utopian monsters, we turn the page, and —

    " ' As thro' the land at eve we went,
        And pluck'd the ripen'd ears,
    We fell out, my wife and I,
    Oh, we fell out, I know not why,
        And kiss'd again with tears.
    And blessings on the falling out
        That all the more endears,
    When we fall out with those we love,
        And kiss again with tears !
    For when we came where lay the child
        We lost in other years,
    There above the little grave,
    Oh, there above the little grave,
        We kiss'd again with tears.'

"Between the next two cantos intervenes the well-known cradle song, perhaps the best of all; and at the next interval is the equally well-known bugle song, the idea of which is that of twin labor and twin fame in a pair of lovers.

"In the next, the memory of wife and child inspirits the soldier in the field; in the next, the sight of the fallen hero's child opens the sluices of his widow's tears; and in the last, and perhaps the most beautiful of all, the poet has succeeded, in the new edition, in superadding a new form of emotion to a canto in which he seemed to have exhausted every resource of pathos which his subject allowed, and prepares us for the triumph of that art by which he makes us, after all, love the heroine whom he at first taught us to hate and despise, till we see that her naughtiness is, after all, one that must be kissed and not whipped out of her, and look on smiling while she repents, with Prince Harry of old, 'not in sackcloth and ashes, but in new silk and old sack.'"

— CHARLES KINGSLEY.

"I rank Tennyson in the first order, because with great mastery over his material — words, great plastic power of versification, and a rare gift of harmony — he has also vision, or insight; and because, feeling intensely the great questions of the day, — not as a mere man of letters, but as a MAN, — he is, to some extent, the interpreter of his age, not only in its mysticism, which I tried to show you is the necessary reaction from the rigid formulas of science and the earthliness of an age of work into the vagueness which belongs to infinitude, but also in his poetic and almost prophetic solution of some of its great questions.

"Thus in his 'Princess,' which he calls a 'Medley,' the former half of which is sportive, and the plot almost too fantastic and impossible for criticism, while the latter portion seems too serious for a story so light and flimsy, he has with exquisite taste disposed of the question — which has its burlesque and comic as well as its tragic side — of woman's present place and future destinies. And if any one wishes to see this subject treated with a masterly and delicate hand, in protest alike against the theories which would make her as the man, which she could only be by becoming masculine, not manly, and those which would have her to remain the toy, or the slave, or the slight thing of sentimental and frivolous accomplishment which education has hitherto aimed at making her, I would recommend him to study the few last pages of 'The Princess,' where the poet brings the question back, as a poet should, to nature; develops the ideal out of the actual woman, and reads out of what she is, on the one hand, what her Creator intended her to be, and on the other, what she never can nor ought to be." — REV. F. W. ROBERTSON.

"'The Princess' is a masterpiece. Exquisite as its author's verse always is, it was never more exquisite than here, whether in blank verse or in the (superadded) lyrics; while none of his deliberately arranged plays contains characters half so good as those of the Princess herself, of Lady Blanche and Lady Psyche, of Cyril, of the two kings, and even of one or two others.

"It may or may not be agreed that the question of the equality of the sexes is one of the distinguishing questions of this century; and some of those who would give it that position may or may not maintain that it is treated here too lightly, while their opponents may wish that it had been treated more lightly still. But this very difference will point the unbiased critic to the same conclusion, that Tennyson has hit 'the golden mean.'"

— GEORGE SAINTSBURY.

"So vividly and clearly does the poet delineate the creatures of his fancy that we cannot help viewing them as actual existences. We find ourselves sympathizing with the Prince, and wishing him success in his arduous suit. We feel the rush of breathless expectation in the hot *mêlée* of the tourney. We wait anxiously the turn of fate beside the sick bed of the wounded lover. It is only when we set ourselves to criticising, that we are struck with the improbability of that which moved us, and become ashamed of our former feelings." — JAMES HADLEY.

"'The Princess' is 'earnest wed to sport' — the attempt of a mind whose feeling for the beautiful and the true is stronger than its humor and fun, to treat certain modern mistakes about the true relation of man and woman with good-humored satire, and in spite of this intention impelled to a strain of serious thought and impassioned feeling. It is a laugh subsiding into tenderness and tears. But, because the commencement is mock heroic, and the machinery highly fanciful, the earnest close seems rather the poet's own utterance of his views of the relations of the sexes than the inherent moral of the story." — GEORGE BRIMLEY.

"Other works of our poet are greater, but none is so fascinating as this romantic tale: English throughout, yet combining the England of Cœur de Leon with that of Victoria in one bewitching picture. 'The Princess' has a distinct purpose — the illustration of woman's struggles, aspirations, and proper sphere; and the conclusion is one wherewith the instincts of cultured people are so thoroughly in accord that some are used to answer, when asked to present their view of the *woman question,* 'You will find it at the close of "The Princess."'"

— EDMUND CLARENCE STEDMAN.

"'The Princess' enshrines the woman's question as it appeared nearly fifty years ago; and, considering all that has been done since then, it is a prophetic utterance. He has touched with grace and clearness a number of the phases of opinion which now prevail, and which then had only begun to prevail, embodying each phase in one of his characters. The woman's question owes a great deal to 'The Princess.'" — STOPFORD A. BROOKE.

"'The Princess' contains Tennyson's solution of the problem of the true position of woman in society, — a profound and vital question upon the solution of which the future of civilization depends. . . . The poem breathes throughout that faith and hope in the future which make Tennyson the poet of a progressive age." — S. E. DAWSON.

TENNYSON'S LETTER ON "THE PRINCESS."

(The following letter was written by Tennyson to Mr. S. E. Dawson soon after the publication of Mr. Dawson's excellent book entitled "A Study of The Princess.")

ALDWORTH, HASLEMERE,
SURREY, Nov. 21, 1882.

DEAR SIR, — I thank you for your able and thoughtful essay on "The Princess." You have seen, amongst other

things that, if women ever were to play such freaks, the
burlesque and the tragic might go hand in hand.

I may tell you that the songs were not an afterthought.
Before the first edition came out I deliberated with myself
whether I should put songs in between the separate divi-
sions of the poem; again, I thought, the poem will explain
itself, but the public did not see that the child, as you say,
was the heroine of the piece, and at last I conquered my
laziness and inserted them.   You would be still more cer-
tain that the child was the true heroine if, instead of the
first song as it now stands,

> " As thro' the land at eve we went,"

I had printed the first song which I wrote, " The Losing of
the Child."   The child is sitting on the bank of a river
and playing with flowers — a flood comes down — a dam
has been broken thro' — the child is borne down by the
flood — the whole village distracted — after a time the
flood has subsided — the child is thrown safe and sound
again upon the bank and all the women are in raptures.
I quite forget the words of the ballad, but I think I may
have it somewhere.

Your explanatory notes are very much to the purpose,
and I do not object to your finding parallelisms.   They
must always recur.   A man (a Chinese scholar) some
time ago wrote to me saying that in an unknown, untrans-
lated Chinese poem there were two whole lines of mine,
almost word for word.   Why not? are not human eyes
all over the world looking at the same objects, and must
there not consequently be coincidences of thought and

impressions and expressions? It is scarcely possible for any one to say or write anything in this late time of the world to which, in the rest of the literature of the world, a parallel could not somewhere be found. But when you say that this passage or that was suggested by Wordsworth, or Shelley, or another, I demur, and more, I wholly disagree. There was a period in my life when, — as an artist, Turner for instance, takes rough sketches of landscape, etc., in order to work them eventually into some great picture, — so I was in the habit of chronicling, in four or five words or more, whatever might strike me as picturesque in nature. I never put these down, and many and many a line has gone away on the north wind, but some remain, *e.g.*,

"A full sea glazed with muffled moonlight."

Suggestion: The sea one night at Torquay, when Torquay was the most lovely sea village in England, tho' now a smoky town. The sky was covered with thin vapor, and the moon was behind it.

"A great black cloud
Drag inward from the deep."

Suggestion: A coming storm seen from the top of Snowdon.

In the "Idylls of the King,"

"with all
Its stormy crests that smote against the skies."

Suggestion: A storm which came upon us in the middle of the North Sea.

> " As the water lily starts and slides."

Suggestion: Water lilies in my own pond, seen on a gusty day with my own eyes. They did start and slide in the sudden puffs of wind, till caught and stayed by the tether of their own stalks — quite as *true* as Wordsworth's simile and more in detail —

> " A wild wind shook —
> Follow, follow, thou shalt win."

Suggestion: I was walking in the New Forest. A wind did arise and

> " Shake the songs, the whispers, and the shrieks
> Of the wild wood together."

The wind, I believe, was a west wind, but, because I wished the Prince to go south, I turned the wind to the south, and, naturally, the wind said "follow." I believe the resemblance which you note is just a chance one. Shelley's lines are not familiar to me, tho', of course, if they occur in the "Prometheus," I must have read them.

I could multiply instances, but I will not bore you, and far indeed am I from asserting that books, as well as nature, are not, and ought not to be, suggestive to the poet. I am sure that I myself, and many others, find a peculiar charm in those passages of such great masters as Virgil or Milton, where they adopt the creation of a bygone poet, and reclothe it, more or less, according to their own fancy. But there is, I fear, a prosaic set growing up among us — editors of booklets, bookworms, index hunters, or men of great memories and no imagination, who *impute themselves* to the poet, and so believe that *he*, too, has no imagination, but is forever poking his nose between the pages of some old volume in order to see what he can appropriate. They will not allow one to say "Ring the bells," without finding that we have taken it from Sir P. Sydney — or even to use such a simple expression as the ocean "roars," without finding out the precise verse in Homer or Horace from which we have plagiarized it (fact!).

I have known an old fishwife, who had lost two sons at sea, clench her fist at the advancing tide on a stormy day, and cry out: "Ay! roar, do! how I hates to see thee show thy white teeth!" Now if I had adopted her exclamation and put it into the mouth of some old woman in one of my poems, I daresay the critics would have thought it original enough, but would most likely have advised me to go to Nature for my old women, and not to my own imagination; and indeed it is a strong figure.

Here is another little anecdote about suggestion. When I was about twenty or twenty-one I went on a tour to the Pyrenees. Lying among these mountains before a waterfall that comes down one thousand or twelve hundred feet, I sketched it (according to my custom then) in these words —

"Slow-dropping veils of thinnest lawn."

When I printed this, a critic informed me that "lawn" was the material used in theaters to imitate a waterfall, and graciously added, 'Mr. T. should not go to the boards of a theater but to Nature herself for his suggestions.' — And I *had* gone to Nature herself.

I think it is a moot point whether, if I had known

how that effect was produced on the stage, I should have ventured to publish the line.

I find that I have written, quite contrary to my custom, a letter, when I had merely intended to thank you for your interesting commentary.

Thanking you again for it, I beg you to believe me

Very faithfully yours,

A. TENNYSON.

P.S. By-the-by, you are wrong about "the tremulous isles of light": they are "isles of light," spots of sunshine coming through the leaves, and seeming to slide from one to the other, as the procession of girls "moves under *shade.*"

And surely the "beard-blown" goat involves a sense of the wind blowing the beard on the height of the ruined pillar.

THE STORY OF "THE PRINCESS."

(Adapted.)

The story of "The Princess" is that of a prince who had been betrothed while yet a child to a child princess in the South. He had in all his growing years worn her portrait and made her his ideal. Upon his coming to manhood, his father, the king, sends an embassy, and claims the maid for his son. But the Princess Ida refuses to marry, having conceived the idea of carrying on a college for women, and educating them to nobler lives than they have led previous to her time.

The Prince determines to seek the Princess, and with two friends from his father's court, and in disguise, he penetrates the retirement of the college. The men are discovered, but are kept from the fate threatened in the sentence upon the gate, "Let no man enter here on pain of death," by the Prince's saving Lady Ida's life in the confusion which follows the disclosure.

The Princess refuses to acknowledge the bond of her betrothal, and calls upon her brothers to vindicate her will. All agree to settle the question by a mediæval tournament, in which fifty knights on either side engage. The Prince is wounded and unhorsed. The Princess, overcome by her love for a child whose fate appeals to her, opens the college to the wounded, sends the students to their homes, and, becoming nurse to the Prince, ends the tale by losing her heart to him and promising marriage.

The scenery of the piece is delightful, full of sunshine, gayety, and grace. The college, with its grounds and high-wrought architecture, courts and gardens, walls and fountains, brightened with glancing girls and silken-clad professors, is charmingly imagined. Nature is not described for her own sake, but inwoven, in Tennyson's manner, with the emotions of those who are looking upon it. The nature touches are chiefly in the comparisons, and this is fitly so, for the human interest is manifold.

Finally, with regard to the poem as distinguished from the social question it speaks of, beauty is kept in it preeminent. It is first in Tennyson's as it ought to be in every artist's heart. The subject-matter is bent to the necessity of beauty. The knowledge displayed in it, the various theories concerning womanhood, the choice of scenery, the events, are all chosen and arranged so as to render it possible to enshrine them in beautiful shapes. This general direction toward loveliness is never lost sight of by the poet. It is not that moral aims are neglected, or the increase of human good, or the heightening of truth, or the declaring of knowledge; but it is that all these things are made subservient to the manifestation of beauty. It is the artist's way, and it is the highest way.

The woman question is not by itself a lovely thing; but it is made beautiful in "The Princess," because every one of its issues is solved by love, by an appeal to some kind of love,—to filial love, to motherly love, to the associated love of friendship, to the high and sacred love between a maiden and her lover, to the natural love which, without particular direction, arises out of pity for the helpless, and to the love we feel for the natural world.

But Tennyson was so exalted by this abiding in love, that he could not help at times in the poem breaking out into lyric songs, in which he might express a keener feeling of beauty, and reach a higher range of poetry than in the rest of the poem. So he wrote in the midst of the poem two love songs,—one, of the sorrow of love passed by forever, of the days that are no more; another, of the joyful hope of love, of the days that are to come. The first of these, "Tears, Idle Tears," represents more nearly than any of the songs of Tennyson, but chiefly in the last verse, one phase, at least, of the passion of love between man and woman. The second song is lovely in movement; its wing-beating and swift-glancing verse is like the flight of the bird that has suggested it. Both songs are unrhymed, yet no one needs the rhyme, so harmoniously is their assonance arranged, not so much at the end of each line as in the body of the lines themselves. "Tears, Idle Tears," is a masterpiece of the careful employment of vowels.

The poet celebrates love, in six of its various phases, in six delightful and happy songs inserted in the third edition between the main divisions of the poem. They were, he says, ballads or songs to give the poets breathing space. They are all of a sweet and gentle humanity, of a fascinating and concentrated brevity, of common moods of human love, made by the poet's sympathy and art to shine like the common stars we love so well. The reconcilement of wife and husband over the grave of their child, the mother singing to her babe of his father coming home from sea, the warrior in battle thinking of his home, the iron grief of the soldier's wife melted at last into tears by his child laid upon her knee, the maiden yielding at last to the love she had kept at bay, — these are the simple subjects of these songs.

Among these the cradle song,

> "Sweet and low, sweet and low,
>   Wind of the western sea,"

is the most beautiful, and writes, as it were, its own music; but the song,

> "The splendor falls on castle walls,
>   And snowy summits old in story,"

is the noblest, — a clear, uplifted, soft, ringing song. These are the songs of this delightful poem.

THE PRINCESS;

A MEDLEY.

———o○⦂⦂○○———

PROLOGUE.

SIR WALTER VIVIAN all a summer's day
Gave his broad lawns until the set of sun
Up to the people: thither flock'd at noon
His tenants, wife and child, and thither half
The neighboring borough with their Institute 5
Of which he was the patron. I was there
From college, visiting the son, — the son
A Walter too, — with others of our set,
Five others: we were seven at Vivian-place.

And me that morning Walter show'd the house, 10
Greek, set with busts: from vases in the hall,
Flowers of all heavens, and lovelier than their names,
Grew side by side; and on the pavement lay
Carved stones of the Abbey ruin in the park,
Huge Ammonites, and the first bones of Time; 15
And on the tables every clime and age
Jumbled together; celts and calumets,
Claymore and snowshoe, toys in lava, fans
Of sandal, amber, ancient rosaries,
Laborious orient ivory sphere in sphere, 20
The cursed Malayan crease, and battle-clubs
From the isles of palm; and higher on the walls,
Betwixt the monstrous horns of elk and deer,
His own forefathers' arms and armor hung.

And "this," he said, "was Hugh's at Agincourt;   2̶
And that was old Sir Ralph's at Ascalon:
A good knight he! we keep a chronicle
With all about him" — which he brought, and I
Dived in a hoard of tales that dealt with knights,
Half-legend, half-historic, counts and kings   30
Who laid about them at their wills and died;
And mixt with these, a lady, one that arm'd
Her own fair head, and sallying thro' the gate,
Had beat her foes with slaughter from her walls.

"O miracle of women," said the book,   35
"O noble heart who, being strait-besieged
By this wild king to force her to his wish,
Nor bent, nor broke, nor shunn'd a soldier's death,
But now when all was lost or seem'd as lost —
Her stature more than mortal in the burst   40
Of sunrise, her arm lifted, eyes on fire —
Brake with a blast of trumpets from the gate,
And, falling on them like a thunderbolt,
She trampled some beneath her horses' heels,
And some were whelm'd with missiles of the wall,   45
And some were push'd with lances from the rock,
And part were drown'd within the whirling brook:
O miracle of noble womanhood!"

So sang the gallant glorious chronicle;
And, I all rapt in this, "Come out," he said,   50
"To the Abbey: there is Aunt Elizabeth
And sister Lilia with the rest." We went
(I kept the book and had my finger in it)
Down thro' the park: strange was the sight to me;
For all the sloping pasture murmur'd, sown   55
With happy faces and with holiday.
There moved the multitude, a thousand heads:
The patient leaders of their Institute

Taught them with facts.   One rear'd a font of stone,
And drew, from butts of water on the slope,   60
The fountain of the moment, playing, now
A twisted snake, and now a rain of pearls,
Or steep-up spout whereon the gilded ball
Danced like a wisp: and somewhat lower down
A man with knobs and wires and vials fired   65
A cannon.   Echo answer'd in her sleep
From hollow fields: and here were telescopes
For azure views; and there a group of girls
In circle waited, whom the electric shock
Dislink'd with shrieks and laughter: round the lake   70
A little clock-work steamer paddling plied,
And shook the lilies: perch'd about the knolls,
A dozen angry models jetted steam:
A petty railway ran: a fire balloon
Rose gem-like up before the dusky groves,   75
And dropt a fairy parachute, and past:
And there thro' twenty posts of telegraph
They flash'd a saucy message to and fro
Between the mimic stations; so that sport
Went hand in hand with science; otherwhere   80
Pure sport: a herd of boys with clamor bowl'd
And stump'd the wicket; babies roll'd about
Like tumbled fruit in grass; and men and maids
Arranged a country dance, and flew thro' light
And shadow, while the twangling violin   85
Struck up with Soldier-laddie, and overhead
The broad ambrosial aisles of lofty lime
Made noise with bees and breeze from end to end.

    Strange was the sight, and smacking of the time;
And long we gazed, but satiated at length   90
Came to the ruins.   High-arch'd and ivy-claspt,
Of finest Gothic lighter than a fire,

Thro' one wide chasm of time and frost they gave
The park, the crowd, the house; but all within
The sward was trim as any garden lawn: 95
And here we lit on Aunt Elizabeth,
And Lilia with the rest, and lady friends
From neighbor seats: and there was Ralph himself,
A broken statue propt against the wall,
As gay as any.   Lilia, wild with sport,   100
Half child, half woman as she was, had wound
A scarf of orange round the stony helm,
And robed the shoulders in a rosy silk,
That made the old warrior from his ivied nook
Glow like a sunbeam: near his tomb a feast   105
Shone, silver-set; about it lay the guests,
And there we join'd them: then the maiden Aunt
Took this fair day for text, and from it preach'd
An universal culture for the crowd,
And all things great; but we, unworthier, told   110
Of college: he had climb'd across the spikes,
And he had squeezed himself betwixt the bars,
And he had breathed the proctor's dogs; and one
Discuss'd his tutor, rough to common men,
But honeying at the whisper of a lord;   115
And one the master, as a rogue in grain
Veneer'd with sanctimonious theory.

But while they talk'd, above their heads I saw
The feudal warrior lady-clad; which brought
My book to mind: and opening this I read   120
Of old Sir Ralph a page or two that rang
With tilt and tourney; then the tale of her
That drove her foes with slaughter from her walls,
And much I praised her nobleness, and "Where,"
Ask'd Walter, patting Lilia's head (she lay   125
Beside him) "lives there such a woman now?"

Quick answer'd Lilia "There are thousands now
Such women, but convention beats them down:
It is but bringing up; no more than that:
You men have done it: how I hate you all!   131
Ah, were I something great! I wish I were
Some mighty poetess, I would shame you then,
That love to keep us children! Oh, I wish
That I were some great princess! I would build
Far off from men a college like a man's,   135
And I would teach them all that men are taught;
We are twice as quick!" And here she shook aside
The hand that play'd the patron with her curls.

And one said, smiling, "Pretty were the sight
If our old halls could change their sex, and flaunt   140
With prudes for proctors, dowagers for deans,
And sweet girl-graduates in their golden hair.
I think they should not wear our rusty gowns,
But move as rich as emperor-moths, or Ralph
Who shines so in the corner; yet I fear,   145
If there were many Lilias in the brood,
However deep you might embower the nest,
Some boy would spy it."
                        At this upon the sward
She tapt her tiny, silken-sandal'd foot:
"That's your light way; but I would make it death   150
For any male thing but to peep at us."

Petulant she spoke, and at herself she laugh'd;
A rosebud set with little wilful thorns,
And sweet as English air could make her, she:
But Walter hail'd a score of names upon her,   155
And "petty Ogress," and "ungrateful Puss,"
And swore he long'd at college, only long'd,
All else was well, for she-society.

They boated and they cricketed; they talk'd
At wine, in clubs, of art, of politics;   160
They lost their weeks; they vext the souls of deans;
They rode; they betted; made a hundred friends,
And caught the blossom of the flying terms,
But miss'd the mignonette of Vivian-place,
The little hearth-flower Lilia.   Thus he spoke,   165
Part banter, part affection.

                "True," she said,
"We doubt not that.   Oh, yes, you miss'd us much;
I'll stake my ruby ring upon it you did!"

  She held it out; and as a parrot turns
Up thro' gilt wires a crafty loving eye,   170
And takes a lady's finger with all care,
And bites it for true heart and not for harm,
So he with Lilia's.   Daintily she shriek'd
And wrung it.   "Doubt my word again!" he said.
"Come, listen! here is proof that you were miss'd: 175
We seven stay'd at Christmas up to read;
And there we took one tutor as to read:
The hard-grain'd Muses of the cube and square
Were out of season: never man, I think,
So molder'd in a sinecure as he: 180
For while our cloisters echo'd frosty feet
And our long walks were stript as bare as brooms,
We did but talk you over, pledge you all
In wassail; often, like as many girls —
Sick for the hollies and the yews of home—   185
As many little trifling Lilias — play'd
Charades and riddles as at Christmas here,
And *what's my thought* and *when* and *where* and *how,*
And often told a tale from mouth to mouth
As here at Christmas."
              She remember'd that: 190

A pleasant game, she thought: she liked it more
Than magic music, forfeits, all the rest.
But these — what kind of tales did men tell men,
She wonder'd, by themselves?

               A half-disdain
Perch'd on the pouted blossom of her lips: 195
And Walter nodded at me; "*He* began,
The rest would follow, each in turn; and so
We forged a sevenfold story. Kind? what kind?
Chimeras, crotchets, Christmas solecisms,
Seven-headed monsters only made to kill   200
Time by the fire in winter."

               "Kill him now,
The tyrant! kill him in the summer too,"
Said Lilia; "Why not now?" the maiden Aunt.
"Why not a summer's as a winter's tale?
A tale for summer as befits the time,   205
And something it should be to suit the place,
Heroic, for a hero lies beneath,
Grave, solemn!"

             Walter warp'd his mouth at this
To something so mock-solemn that I laugh'd,
And Lilia woke with sudden-shrilling mirth   210
An echo like a ghostly woodpecker,
Hid in the ruins; till the maiden Aunt
(A little sense of wrong had touch'd her face
With color) turn'd to me with, "As you will;
Heroic if you will, or what you will,   215
Or be yourself your hero if you will."

   "Take Lilia, then, for heroine," clamor'd he,
"And make her some great Princess, six feet high,
Grand, epic, homicidal; and be you
The Prince to win her!"

            "Then follow me, the Prince," 220

I answer'd; "each be hero in his turn!
Seven and yet one, like shadows in a dream. —
Heroic seems our Princess as required —
But something made to suit with time and place,
A Gothic ruin and a Grecian house,   225
A talk of college and of ladies' rights,
A feudal knight in silken masquerade,
And, yonder, shrieks and strange experiments
For which the good Sir Ralph had burnt them all —
This *were* a medley! we should have him back   230
Who told the 'Winter's Tale' to do it for us.
No matter: we will say whatever comes.
And let the ladies sing us, if they will,
From time to time, some ballad or a song
To give us breathing-space."
                    So I began,   235
And the rest follow'd: and the women sang
Between the rougher voices of the men,
Like linnets in the pauses of the wind:
And here I give the story and the songs.

CANTO I.

A prince I was, blue-eyed, and fair in face,
Of temper amorous, as the first of May,
With lengths of yellow ringlet, like a girl,
For on my cradle shone the Northern star.

There lived an ancient legend in our house.   5
Some sorcerer, whom a far-off grandsire burnt
Because he cast no shadow, had foretold,
Dying, that none of all our blood should know
The shadow from the substance, and that one
Should come to fight with shadows and to fall.   10
For so, my mother said, the story ran.

And, truly, waking dreams were, more or less,
An old and strange affection of the house.
Myself too had weird seizures, Heaven knows what:
On a sudden in the midst of men and day,   15
And while I walk'd and talk'd as heretofore,
I seem'd to move among a world of ghosts,
And feel myself the shadow of a dream.
Our great court-Galen poised his gilt-head cane,
And paw'd his beard, and mutter'd "catalepsy."   20
My mother pitying made a thousand prayers, —
My mother was as mild as any saint,
Half-canonized by all that look'd on her,
So gracious was her tact and tenderness.
But my good father thought a king a king;   25
He cared not for the affection of the house;
He held his scepter like a pedant's wand
To lash offense, and with long arms and hands
Reach'd out, and pick'd offenders from the mass
For judgment.
                    Now it chanced that I had been,   30
While life was yet in bud and blade, betroth'd
To one, a neighboring Princess: she to me
Was proxy-wedded with a bootless calf
At eight years old; and still from time to time
Came murmurs of her beauty from the South,   35
And of her brethren, youths of puissance;
And still I wore her picture by my heart,
And one dark tress; and all around them both
Sweet thoughts would swarm as bees about their queen.

But when the days drew nigh that I should wed,   40
My father sent ambassadors with furs
And jewels, gifts, to fetch her: these brought back
A present, a great labor of the loom;
And therewithal an answer vague as wind:

Besides, they saw the king; he took the gifts;   **45**
He said there was a compact; that was true:
But then she had a will; was he to blame?
And maiden fancies; loved to live alone
Among her women; certain, would not wed.

    That morning in the presence room I stood   **50**
With Cyril and with Florian, my two friends:
The first, a gentleman of broken means
(His father's fault), but given to starts and bursts
Of revel; and the last, my other heart,
And almost my half-self, for still we moved   **55**
Together, twinn'd as horse's ear and eye.

    Now, while they spake, I saw my father's face
Grow long and troubled like a rising moon,
Inflamed with wrath: he started on his feet,
Tore the king's letter, snow'd it down, and rent   **60**
The wonder of the loom thro' warp and woof
From skirt to skirt; and at the last he sware
That he would send a hundred thousand men,
And bring her in a whirlwind: then he chew'd
The thrice-turn'd cud of wrath, and cook'd his spleen,   **65**
Communing with his captains of the war.

    At last I spoke. "My father, let me go.
It cannot be but some gross error lies
In this report, this answer of a king,
Whom all men rate as kind and hospitable: **70**
Or, maybe, I myself, my bride once seen,
Whate'er my grief to find her less than fame,
May rue the bargain made."   And Florian said:
"I have a sister at the foreign court,
Who moves about the Princess; she, you know,   **75**
Who wedded with a nobleman from thence:

He, dying lately, left her, as I hear,
The lady of three castles in that land:
Thro' her this matter might be sifted clean."
And Cyril whisper'd: "Take me with you, too." 80
Then, laughing, "what, if these weird seizures come
Upon you in those lands, and no one near
To point you out the shadow from the truth!
Take me: I'll serve you better in a strait;
I grate on rusty hinges here:" but, "No!" 85
Roar'd the rough king, "you shall not; we ourself
Will crush her pretty maiden fancies dead
In iron gauntlets: break the council up."

But when the council broke, I rose and past
Thro' the wild woods that hung about the town; 90
Found a still place, and pluck'd her likeness out;
Laid it on flowers, and watch'd it lying bathed
In the green gleam of dewy-tassel'd trees:
What were those fancies? wherefore break her troth?
Proud look'd the lips: but, while I meditated, 95
A wind arose and rush'd upon the South,
And shook the songs, the whispers, and the shrieks
Of the wild woods together; and a Voice
Went with it, "Follow, follow, thou shalt win."

Then, ere the silver sickle of that month 100
Became her golden shield, I stole from court
With Cyril and with Florian, unperceived,
Cat-footed thro' the town, and half in dread
To hear my father's clamor at our backs
With "Ho!" from some bay-window shake the night; 105
But all was quiet: from the bastion'd walls
Like threaded spiders, one by one, we dropt,
And flying reach'd the frontier: then we crost
To a livelier land; and so by tilth and grange,

And vines, and blowing bosks of wilderness,   110
We gain'd the mother-city thick with towers,
And in the imperial palace found the king.

  His name was Gama; crack'd and small his voice,
But bland the smile that like a wrinkling wind
On glassy water drove his cheek in lines;   115
A little dry old man, without a star,
Not like a king; three days he feasted us,
And on the fourth I spake of why we came,
And my betroth'd.   "You do us, Prince," he said,
Airing a snowy hand and signet gem,   120
"All honor.   We remember love ourselves
In our sweet youth : there did a compact pass
Long summers back, a kind of ceremony —
I think the year in which our olives fail'd.
I would you had her, Prince, with all my heart,   125
With my full heart: but there were widows here,
Two widows, Lady Psyche, Lady Blanche;
They fed her theories, in and out of place
Maintaining that with equal husbandry
The woman were an equal to the man.   130
They harp'd on this; with this our banquets rang;
Our dances broke and buzz'd in knots of talk;
Nothing but this; my very ears were hot
To hear them: knowledge, so my daughter held,
Was all in all: they had but been, she thought,   135
As children; they must lose the child, assume
The woman: then, Sir, awful odes she wrote,
Too awful, sure, for what they treated of,
But all she is and does is awful; odes
About this losing of the child; and rhymes   140
And dismal lyrics, prophesying change
Beyond all reason: these the women sang;
And they that know such things — I sought but peace;

No critic I — would call them masterpieces:
They master'd *me*.   At last she begg'd a boon,   145
A certain summer palace which I have
Hard by your father's frontier: I said no,
Yet, being an easy man, gave it: and there,
All wild to found an University
For maidens, on the spur she fled; and more   150
We know not, — only this: they see no men,
Not ev'n her brother Arac, nor the twins
Her brethren, tho' they love her, look upon her
As on a kind of paragon; and I
(Pardon me saying it) were much loth to breed   155
Dispute betwixt myself and mine: but since
(And I confess with right) you think me bound
In some sort, I can give you letters to her;
And yet, to speak the truth, I rate your chance
Almost at naked nothing."

                      Thus the king: 160
And I, tho' nettled that he seem'd to slur
With garrulous ease and oily courtesies
Our formal compact, yet, not less (all frets
But chafing me on fire to find my bride)
Went forth again with both my friends.   We rode   165
Many a long league back to the North.   At last,
From hills that look'd across a land of hope,
We dropt with evening on a rustic town
Set in a gleaming river's crescent curve,
Close at the boundary of the liberties;   170
There, enter'd an old hostel, call'd mine host
To council, plied him with his richest wines,
And show'd the late-writ letters of the king.

  He with a long low sibilation, stared
As blank as death in marble; then exclaim'd,   175
Averring it was clear against all rules

For any man to go; but as his brain
Began to mellow, "If the king," he said,
"Had given us letters, was he bound to speak?
The king would bear him out"; and at the last — 180
The summer of the vine in all his veins —
"No doubt that we might make it worth his while.
She once had past that way; he heard her speak;
She scared him; life! he never saw the like;
She look'd as grand as doomsday and as grave: 185
And he, he reverenced his liege lady there;
He always made a point to post with mares;
His daughter and his housemaid were the boys:
The land, he understood, for miles about
Was till'd by women; all the swine were sows, 190
And all the dogs" —
                            But while he jested thus,
A thought flash'd thro' me which I clothed in act,
Remembering how we three presented Maid
Or Nymph, or Goddess, at high tide of feast,
In masque or pageant at my father's court. 195
We sent mine host to purchase female gear;
He brought it, and himself, a sight to shake
The midriff of despair with laughter, holp
To lace us up, till, each, in maiden plumes
We rustled: him we gave a costly bribe 200
To guerdon silence, mounted our good steeds,
And boldly ventured on the liberties.

We follow'd up the river as we rode,
And rode till midnight when the college lights
Began to glitter firefly-like in copse 205
And linden alley: then we past an arch,
Whereon a woman-statue rose with wings
From four wing'd horses dark against the stars;
And some inscription ran along the front,

But deep in shadow : further on we gain'd   210
A little street, half garden and half house ;
But scarce could hear each other speak for noise
Of clocks and chimes, like silver hammers falling
On silver anvils, and the splash and stir
Of fountains spouted up and showering down   215
In meshes of the jasmine and the rose :
And all about us peal'd the nightingale,
Rapt in her song, and careless of the snare.

There stood a bust of Pallas for a sign,
By two sphere lamps, blazon'd like Heaven and Earth   220
With constellation and with continent,
Above an entry : riding in, we call'd ;
A plump-arm'd ostleress, and a stable wench
Came running at the call, and help'd us down.
Then stept a buxom hostess forth, and sail'd,   225
Full-blown, before us into rooms which gave
Upon a pillar'd porch, the bases lost
In laurel : her we ask'd of that and this,
And who were tutors. " Lady Blanche," she said,
" And Lady Psyche." " Which was prettiest,   230
Best-natured ? " " Lady Psyche." " Hers are we,"
One voice, we cried ; and I sat down and wrote,
In such a hand as when a field of corn
Bows all its ears before the roaring East :

" Three ladies of the Northern empire pray   235
Your Highness would enroll them with your own,
As Lady Psyche's pupils." This I seal'd :
The seal was Cupid bent above a scroll,
And o'er his head Uranian Venus hung,
And raised the blinding bandage from his eyes :   240
I gave the letter to be sent with dawn ;
And then to bed, where half in doze I seem'd

To float about a glimmering night, and watch
A full sea, glaz'd with muffled moonlight, swell
On some dark shore just seen that it was rich.   245

————————

> As thro' the land at eve we went,
>   And pluck'd the ripen'd ears,
> We fell out, my wife and I,
> Oh, we fell out, I know not why,
>   And kiss'd again with tears.
> And blessings on the falling out
>   That all the more endears,
> When we fall out with those we love
>   And kiss again with tears !
> For when we came where lay the child
>   We lost in other years,
> There above the little grave,
> Oh, there above the little grave,
>   We kiss'd again with tears !

————————

CANTO II.

At break of day the college portress came:
She brought us Academic silks, in hue
The lilac, with a silken hood to each,
And zoned with gold; and now when these were on,
And we as rich as moths from dusk cocoons,   5
She, curtseying her obeisance, let us know
The Princess Ida waited: out we paced,
I first, and following thro' the porch that sang
All round with laurel, issued in a court
Compact of lucid marbles, boss'd with lengths   10
Of classic frieze, with ample awnings gay
Betwixt the pillars, and with great urns of flowers.
The Muses and the Graces, group'd in threes,
Enring'd a billowing fountain in the midst;

And here and there on lattice edges lay 15
Or book or lute; but hastily we past,
And up a flight of stairs into the hall.
There at a board by tome and paper sat,
With two tame leopards couch'd beside her throne,
All beauty compass'd in a female form, 20
The Princess; liker to the inhabitant
Of some clear planet close upon the Sun,
Than our man's earth; such eyes were in her head,
And so much grace and power, breathing down
From over her arch'd brows, with every turn 25
Lived thro' her to the tips of her long hands,
And to her feet. She rose her height, and said:

  "We give you welcome: not without redound
Of use and glory to yourselves ye come,
The first-fruits of the stranger: aftertime, 30
And that full voice which circles round the grave,
Will rank you nobly, mingled up with me.
What! are the ladies of your land so tall?" really men
"We of the court," said Cyril. "From the court,"
She answer'd, "then ye know the Prince?" And he: 35
"The climax of his age! as tho' there were
One rose in all the world, your highness that,
He worships your ideal." She replied:
"We scarcely thought in our own hall to hear
This barren verbiage, current among men, 40
Light coin, the tinsel clink of compliment.
Your flight from out your bookless wilds would seem
As arguing love of knowledge and of power;
Your language proves you still the child. Indeed,
We dream not of him: when we set our hand 45
To this great work, we purposed with ourself
Never to wed. You likewise will do well,
Ladies, in entering here, to cast and fling

The tricks, which make us toys of men, that so,
Some future time, if so indeed you will,   50
You may with those self-styled our lords ally
Your fortunes, justlier balanced, scale with scale."

    At those high words, we, conscious of ourselves,
Perused the matting; then an officer
Rose up and read the statutes, such as these: 55
Not for three years to correspond with home;
Not for three years to cross the liberties;
Not for three years to speak with any men;
And many more, which, hastily subscribed,
We enter'd on the boards: and "Now," she cried,   60
"Ye are green wood, see ye warp not. Look, our hall!
Our statues! — not of those that men desire,
Sleek Odalisques, or oracles of mode,
Nor stunted squaws of West or East; but she
That taught the Sabine how to rule, and she,   65
The foundress of the Babylonian wall,
The Carian Artemisia strong in war,
The Rhodope, that built the pyramid,
Clelia, Cornelia, with the Palmyrene
That fought Aurelian, and the Roman brows   70
Of Agrippina.   Dwell with these, and lose
Convention, since to look on noble forms
Makes noble thro' the sensuous organism
That which is higher.   Oh, lift your natures up:
Embrace our aims: work out your freedom.   Girls,   75
Knowledge is now no more a fountain seal'd:
Drink deep, until the habits of the slave,
The sins of emptiness, gossip and spite
And slander, die.   Better not be at all
Than not be noble.   Leave us: you may go: 80
To-day the Lady Psyche will harangue
The fresh arrivals of the week before;

For they press in from all the provinces,
And fill the hive."
                              She spoke, and bowing waved
Dismissal: back again we crost the court   85
To Lady Psyche's: as we enter'd in,
There sat along the forms, like morning doves
That sun their milky bosoms on the thatch,
A patient range of pupils; she herself
Erect behind a desk of satinwood,   90
A quick brunette, well-molded, falcon-eyed,
And on the hither side, or so she look'd,
Of twenty summers. At her left, a child,
In shining draperies, headed like a star,
Her maiden babe, a double April old,   95
Aglaia slept. We sat: the Lady glanced:
Then Florian, but no livelier than the dame
That whisper'd "Asses' ears" among the sedge,
"My sister." "Comely, too, by all that's fair,"
Said Cyril. "Oh, hush, hush!" and she began.   100

"This world was once a fluid haze of light,
Till toward the center set the starry tides,
And eddied into suns that, wheeling, cast
The planets: then the monster, then the man;
Tattoo'd or woaded, winter-clad in skins,   105
Raw from the prime, and crushing down his mate,
As yet we find in barbarous isles, and here
Among the lowest."
                              Thereupon she took
A bird's-eye view of all the ungracious past;
Glanced at the legendary Amazon   110
As emblematic of a nobler age;
Appraised the Lycian custom, spoke of those
That lay at wine with Lar and Lucumo;
Ran down the Persian, Grecian, Roman lines

Of empire, and the woman's state in each,   115
How far from just; till, warming with her theme,
She fulmined out her scorn of laws Salique
And little-footed China, touch'd on Mahomet
With much contempt, and came to chivalry:
When some respect, however slight, was paid   120
To woman, superstition all awry:
However then commenced the dawn: a beam
Had slanted forward, falling in a land
Of promise; fruit would follow.   Deep, indeed,
Their debt of thanks to her who first had dared   125
To leap the rotten pales of prejudice,
Disyoke their necks from custom, and assert
None lordlier than themselves but that which made
Woman and man.   She had founded; they must build.
Here might they learn whatever men were taught: 130
Let them not fear: some said their heads were less:
Some men's were small; not they the least of men;
For often fineness compensated size:
Besides the brain was like the hand, and grew
With using; thence the man's, if more was more;   135
He took advantage of his strength to be
First in the field: some ages had been lost;
But woman ripen'd earlier, and her life
Was longer; and albeit their glorious names
Were fewer, scatter'd stars, yet since in truth   140
The highest is the measure of the man,
And not the Kaffir, Hottentot, Malay,
Nor those horn-handed breakers of the glebe,
But Homer, Plato, Verulam; even so
With woman: and in arts of government,   145
Elizabeth and others; arts of war,
The peasant Joan and others; arts of grace,
Sappho and others vied with any man:
And, last not least, she who had left her place,

And bow'd her state to them, that they might grow   150
To use and power on this Oasis, lapt
In the arms of leisure, sacred from the blight
Of ancient influence and scorn.
                                    At last
She rose upon a wind of prophecy,
Dilating on the future: "everywhere   155
Two heads in council, two beside the hearth,
Two in the tangled business of the world,
Two in the liberal offices of life,
Two plummets dropt for one to sound the abyss
Of science, and the secrets of the mind: 160
Musician, painter, sculptor, critic, more:
And everywhere the broad and bounteous Earth
Should bear a double growth of those rare souls,
Poets, whose thoughts enrich the blood of the world."

    She ended here, and beckon'd us: the rest   165
Parted; and, glowing full-faced welcome, she
Began to address us, and was moving on
In gratulation, till as when a boat
Tacks, and the slacken'd sail flaps, all her voice
Faltering and fluttering in her throat, she cried,   170
"My brother!" "Well, my sister." "Oh," she said,
"What do you here? and in this dress? and these?
Why who are these? a wolf within the fold!
A pack of wolves! the Lord be gracious to me!
A plot, a plot, a plot, to ruin all!"   175
"No plot, no plot," he answer'd. "Wretched boy,
How saw you not the inscription on the gate,
'LET NO MAN ENTER IN ON PAIN OF DEATH'?"
"And if I had," he answer'd, "who could think
The softer Adams of your Academe,   180
O sister, Sirens tho' they be, were such
As chanted on the blanching bones of men?"

"But you will find it otherwise," she said.
"You jest: ill jesting with edge-tools! my vow
Binds me to speak, and oh that iron will,   184
That ax-like edge unturnable, our Head,
The Princess!"   "Well then, Psyche, take my life,
And nail me like a weasel on a grange
For warning: bury me beside the gate,
And cut this epitaph above my bones, —   190
Here lies a brother by a sister slain,
All for the common good of womankind."
"Let me die too," said Cyril, "having seen
And heard the Lady Psyche."

                    I struck in:
"Albeit so mask'd, Madam, I love the truth;   195
Receive it; and in me behold the Prince
Your countryman, affianced years ago
To the Lady Ida: here, for here she was,
And thus (what other way was left) I came."
"O Sir, O Prince! I have no country; none;   200
If any, this; but none.   Whate'er I was
Disrooted, what I am is grafted here.
Affianced, Sir? love-whispers may not breathe
Within this vestal limit, and how should I,
Who am not mine, say, live: the thunderbolt   205
Hangs silent; but prepare: I speak; it falls."
"Yet pause," I said: "for that inscription there,
I think no more of deadly lurks therein,
Than in a clapper clapping in a garth,
To scare the fowl from fruit: if more there be,   210
If more and acted on, what follows? war;
Your own work marr'd: for this your Academe,
Whichever side be victor, in the halloo
Will topple to the trumpet down, and pass
With all fair theories only made to gild   215
A stormless summer."   "Let the Princess judge

Of that," she said: "farewell, Sir — and to you.
I shudder at the sequel, but I go."

  "Are you that Lady Psyche," I rejoin'd,
"The fifth in line from that old Florian,   220
Yet hangs his portrait in my father's hall
(The gaunt old Baron with his beetle brow
Sun-shaded in the heat of dusty fights),
As he bestrode my Grandsire when he fell,
And all else fled?   We point to it, and we say,   225
'The loyal warmth of Florian is not cold,
But branches current yet in kindred veins.'"
"Are you that Psyche," Florian added; "she
With whom I sang about the morning hills,
Flung ball, flew kite, and raced the purple fly,   230
And snared the squirrel of the glen? are you
That Psyche, wont to bind my throbbing brow,
To smooth my pillow, mix the foaming draught
Of fever, tell me pleasant tales, and read
My sickness down to happy dreams? are you   235
That brother-sister Psyche, both in one?
You were that Psyche, but what are you now?"
"You are that Psyche," Cyril said, "for whom
I would be that for ever which I seem,
Woman, if I might sit beside your feet,   240
And glean your scatter'd sapience."
                              Then once more,
"Are you that Lady Psyche," I began,
"That on her bridal morn, before she past
From all her old companions, when the king
Kiss'd her pale cheek, declared that ancient ties   245
Would still be dear beyond the southern hills;
That were there any of our people there
In want or peril, there was one to hear
And help them? Look! for such are these and I."

"Are you that Psyche," Florian ask'd, "to whom,   250
In gentler days, your arrow-wounded fawn
Came flying while you sat beside the well?
The creature laid his muzzle on your lap,
And sobb'd and you sobb'd with it, and the blood
Was sprinkled on your kirtle, and you wept.   255
That was fawn's blood, not brother's, yet you wept.
Oh, by the bright head of my little niece,
You were that Psyche, and what are you now?"
"You are that Psyche," Cyril said again,
"The mother of the sweetest little maid,   260
That ever crow'd for kisses."

                        "Out upon it!"
She answer'd, "peace! and why should I not play
The Spartan Mother with emotion, be
The Lucius Junius Brutus of my kind?
Him you call great: he for the common weal,   265
The fading politics of mortal Rome,
As I might slay this child, if good need were,
Slew both his sons: and I, shall I, on whom
The secular emancipation turns
Of half this world, be swerved from right to save   270
A prince, a brother? a little will I yield.
Best so, perchance, for us, and well for you.
Oh hard, when love and duty clash! I fear
My conscience will not count me fleckless; yet—
Hear my conditions. promise (otherwise   275
You perish), as you came, to slip away
To-day, to-morrow, soon: it shall be said,
These women were too barbarous, would not learn;
They fled, who might have shamed us: promise all."

   What could we else, we promised each; and she,   280
Like some wild creature newly caged, commenced
A to-and-fro, so pacing till she paused

By Florian; holding out her lily arms,
Took both his hands, and smiling faintly said:
"I knew you at the first: tho' you have grown   285
You scarce have alter'd: I am sad and glad
To see you, Florian.   *I* give thee to death,
My brother! it was duty spoke, not I.
My needful seeming harshness, pardon it.
Our mother, is she well?"

                              With that she kiss'd   290
His forehead, then, a moment after, clung
About him, and betwixt them blossom'd up
From out a common vein of memory
Sweet household talk, and phrases of the hearth,
And far allusion, till the gracious dews   295
Began to glisten and to fall: and while
They stood, so rapt, we gazing, came a voice,
"I brought a message here from Lady Blanche."
Back started she, and turning round we saw
The Lady Blanche's daughter where she stood,   300
Melissa, with her hand upon the lock,
A rosy blonde, and in a college gown
That clad her like an April daffodilly
(Her mother's color), with her lips apart,
And all her thoughts as fair within her eyes   305
As bottom agates seen to wave and float
In crystal currents of clear morning seas.

  So stood that same fair creature at the door.
Then Lady Psyche, "Ah — Melissa — you!
You heard us?" And Melissa, "Oh, pardon me!   310
I heard, I could not help it, did not wish:
But, dearest Lady, pray you fear me not,
Nor think I bear that heart within my breast,
To give three gallant gentlemen to death."
"I trust you," said the other, "for we two   315

Were always friends, none closer, elm and vine:
But yet your mother's jealous temperament —
Let not your prudence, dearest, drowse, or prove
The Danaïd of a leaky vase, for fear
This whole foundation ruin, and I lose   320
My honor, these their lives." "Ah, fear me not,"
Replied Melissa; "no — I would not tell,
No, not for all Aspasia's cleverness,
No, not to answer, Madam, all those hard things
That Sheba came to ask of Solomon."   325
"Be it so," the other, "that we still may lead
The new light up, and culminate in peace,
For Solomon may come to Sheba yet."
Said Cyril, "Madam, he the wisest man
Feasted the woman wisest then, in halls   330
Of Lebanonian cedar: nor should you
(Tho', Madam, *you* should answer, *we* would ask)
Less welcome find among us if you came
Among us, debtors for our lives to you,
Myself for something more." He said not what,   335
But, "Thanks," she answer'd, "Go: we have been too long
Together: keep your hoods about the face;
They do so that affect abstraction here.
Speak little; mix not with the rest; and hold
Your promise: all, I trust, may yet be well."   340

We turn'd to go, but Cyril took the child,
And held her round the knees against his waist,
And blew the swoll'n cheek of a trumpeter,
While Psyche watch'd them, smiling, and the child
Push'd her flat hand against his face and laugh'd;   345
And thus our conference closed.

                        And then we stroll'd
For half the day thro' stately theaters
Bench'd crescent-wise. In each we sat, we heard

The grave Professor.   On the lecture slate
The circle rounded under female hands   350
With flawless demonstration: follow'd then
A classic lecture, rich in sentiment,
With scraps of thundrous Epic lilted out
By violet-hooded Doctors, elegies
And quoted odes, and jewels five-words-long   355
That on the stretch'd forefinger of all Time
Sparkle for ever: then we dipt in all
That treats of whatsoever is, the state,
The total chronicles of man, the mind,
The morals, something of the frame, the rock,   360
The star, the bird, the fish, the shell, the flower,
Electric, chemic laws, and all the rest,
And whatsoever can be taught and known;
Till, like three horses that have broken fence,
And glutted all night long breast-deep in corn,   365
We issued gorged with knowledge, and I spoke:
"Why, Sirs, they do all this as well as we."
"They hunt old trails," said Cyril, "very well;
But when did woman ever yet invent?"
"Ungracious!" answer'd Florian; "have you learnt   370
No more from Psyche's lecture, you that talk'd
The trash that made me sick, and almost sad?"
"Oh, trash," he said, "but with a kernel in it.
Should I not call her wise, who made me wise?
And learnt?   I learnt more from her in a flash,   375
Than if my brainpan were an empty hull,
And every Muse tumbled a science in.
A thousand hearts lie fallow in these halls,
And round these halls a thousand baby loves
Fly twanging headless arrows at the hearts,   380
Whence follows many a vacant pang; but oh!
With me, Sir, enter'd in the bigger boy,
The Head of all the golden-shafted firm,

The long-limb'd lad that had a Psyche too;
He cleft me thro' the stomacher; and now   385
What think you of it, Florian? do I chase
The substance or the shadow? will it hold?
I have no sorcerer's malison on me,
No ghostly hauntings like his Highness.   I
Flatter myself that always everywhere   390
I know the substance when I see it.   Well,
Are castles shadows?   Three of them?   Is she
The sweet proprietress a shadow?   If not,
Shall those three castles patch my tatter'd coat?
For dear are those three castles to my wants,   395
And dear is sister Psyche to my heart,
And two dear things are one of double worth,
And much I might have said, but that my zone
Unmann'd me: then the Doctors!   Oh, to hear
The Doctors!   Oh, to watch the thirsty plants   400
Imbibing!   Once or twice I thought to roar,
To break my chain, to shake my mane: but thou
Modulate me, Soul of mincing mimicry!
Make liquid treble of that bassoon, my throat;
Abase those eyes that ever loved to meet   405
Star-sisters answering under crescent brows;
Abate the stride, which speaks of man, and loose
A flying charm of blushes o'er this cheek,
Where they like swallows coming out of time
Will wonder why they came: but hark, the bell   410
For dinner, let us go!"
                              And in we stream'd
Among the columns, pacing staid and still
By twos and threes, till all from end to end
With beauties every shade of brown and fair
In colors gayer than the morning mist,   415
The long hall glitter'd like a bed of flowers.
How might a man not wander from his wits

Pierced thro' with eyes, but that I kept mine own
Intent on her, who rapt in glorious dreams,
The second-sight of some Astræan age,   420
Sat compass'd with professors! they, the while,
Discuss'd a doubt and tost it to and fro:
A clamor thicken'd, mixt with inmost terms
Of art and science: Lady Blanche alone
Of faded form and haughtiest lineaments,   425
With all her autumn tresses falsely brown,
Shot sidelong daggers at us, a tiger-cat
In act to spring. At last a solemn grace
Concluded, and we sought the gardens: there
One walk'd reciting by herself, and one   430
In this hand held a volume as to read,
And smoothed a petted peacock down with that:
Some to a low song oar'd a shallop by,
Or under arches of the marble bridge
Hung, shadow'd from the heat: some hid and sought   435
In the orange thickets: others tost a ball
Above the fountain jets and back again,
With laughter: others lay about the lawns,
Of the older sort, and murmur'd that their May
Was passing: what was learning unto them?   440
They wish'd to marry; they could rule a house;
Men hated learned women: but we three
Sat muffled like the Fates; and often came
Melissa hitting all we saw with shafts
Of gentle satire, kin to charity,   445
That harm'd not: then day droopt; the chapel bells
Call'd us: we left the walks; we mixt with those
Six hundred maidens clad in purest white,
Before two streams of light from wall to wall,
While the great organ almost burst his pipes,   450
Groaning for power, and rolling thro' the court
A long melodious thunder to the sound

Of solemn psalms, and silver litanies,
The work of Ida, to call down from Heaven
A blessing on her labors for the world.   455

———————

Sweet and low, sweet and low,
   Wind of the western sea,
Low, low, breathe and blow,
   Wind of the western sea !
Over the rolling waters go,
Come from the dying moon, and blow,
   Blow him again to me ;
While my little one, while my pretty one, sleeps.

Sleep and rest, sleep and rest,
   Father will come to thee soon ;
Rest, rest, on mother's breast,
   Father will come to thee soon ;
Father will come to his babe in the nest,
Silver sails all out of the west
   Under the silver moon :
Sleep, my little one, sleep, my pretty one, sleep.

———————

Canto III.

Morn in the white wake of the morning star
Came furrowing all the orient into gold.
We rose, and each by other drest with care
Descended to the court that lay three parts
In shadow, but the Muses' heads were touch'd   5
Above the darkness from their native East.
There while we stood beside the fount, and watch'd
Or seem'd to watch the dancing bubble, approach'd
Melissa, tinged with wan from lack of sleep,
Or grief, and glowing round her dewy eyes   10
The circled Iris of a night of tears ;
"And fly," she cried, "oh, fly while yet you may !
My mother knows :" and when I ask'd her "How ?"

"My fault," she wept, "my fault! and yet not mine;
Yet mine in part. Oh, hear me, pardon me! 15
My mother, 'tis her wont from night to night
To rail at Lady Psyche and her side.
She says the Princess should have been the Head,
Herself and Lady Psyche the two arms;
And so it was agreed when first they came; 20
But Lady Psyche was the right hand now,
And she the left, or not, or seldom used;
Hers more than half the students, all the love.
And so last night she fell to canvass you:
Her countrywomen! she did not envy her. 25
'Who ever saw such wild barbarians?
Girls? — more like men!' and at these words the snake,
My secret, seem'd to stir within my breast;
And oh, Sirs, could I help it, but my cheek
Began to burn and burn, and her lynx eye 30
To fix and make me hotter, till she laugh'd:
'O marvelously modest maiden, you!
Men! girls, like men! why, if they had been men,
You need not set your thoughts in rubric thus
For wholesale comment.' Pardon, I am ashamed 35
That I must needs repeat for my excuse
What looks so little graceful: 'men' (for still
My mother went revolving on the word),
'And so they are, — very like men indeed —
And with that woman closeted for hours!' 40
Then came these dreadful words out one by one,
'Why — these — *are* — men': I shudder'd: 'and you know
    it.'
'Oh, ask me nothing,' I said: 'And she knows too,
And she conceals it.' So my mother clutch'd
The truth at once, but with no word from me; 45
And now thus early risen she goes to inform
The Princess: Lady Psyche will be crush'd;

But you may yet be saved, and therefore fly:
But heal me with your pardon ere you go."

    "What pardon, sweet Melissa, for a blush?"   50
Said Cyril: "Pale one, blush again: than wear
Those lilies, better blush our lives away.
Yet let us breathe for one hour more in Heaven,"
He added, "lest some classic Angel speak
In scorn of us, 'They mounted, Ganymedes,   55
To tumble, Vulcans, on the second morn.'
But I will melt this marble into wax
To yield us farther furlough:" and he went.

    Melissa shook her doubtful curls, and thought
He scarce would prosper. "Tell us," Florian ask'd,   60
"How grew this feud betwixt the right and left."
"Oh, long ago," she said, "betwixt these two
Division smolders hidden; 'tis my mother,
Too jealous, often fretful as the wind
Pent in a crevice: much I bear with her: 65
I never knew my father, but she says
(God help her) she was wedded to a fool;
And still she rail'd against the state of things.
She had the care of Lady Ida's youth,
And from the Queen's decease she brought her up.   70
But when your sister came, she won the heart
Of Ida: they were still together, grew
(For so they said themselves) inosculated;
Consonant chords that shiver to one note;
One mind in all things: yet my mother still   75
Affirms your Psyche thieved her theories,
And angled with them for her pupil's love:
She calls her plagiarist; I know not what:
But I must go: I dare not tarry," and, light
As flies the shadow of a bird, she fled.   80

Then murmur'd Florian gazing after her,
" An open-hearted maiden, true and pure.
If I could love, why this were she: how pretty
Her blushing was, and now she blush'd again
As if to close with Cyril's random wish: 85
Not like your Princess cramm'd with erring pride,
Nor like poor Psyche whom she drags in tow."

" The crane," I said, " may chatter of the crane,
The dove may murmur of the dove, but I
An eagle clang an eagle to the sphere.   90
My princess, O my princess! true she errs,
But in her own grand way: being herself
Three times more noble than three score of men,
She sees herself in every woman else,
And so she wears her error like a crown   95
To blind the truth and me: for her, and her
Hebes are they to hand ambrosia, mix
The nectar; but — ah she — whene'er she moves,
The Samian Herè rises, and she speaks —
A Memnon smitten with the morning Sun."   100

So saying, from the court we paced, and gain'd
The terrace ranged along the Northern front,
And, leaning there on those balusters, high
Above the empurpled champaign, drank the gale
That, blown about the foliage underneath,   105
And sated with the innumerable rose,
Beat balm upon our eyelids.   Hither came
Cyril, and yawning, " O hard task," he cried;
" No fighting shadows here!   I forced a way
Thro' solid opposition crabb'd and gnarl'd.   110
Better to clear prime forests, heave and thump
A league of street in summer solstice down,
Than hammer at this reverend gentlewoman.

I knock'd and, bidden, enter'd; found her there
At point to move, and settled in her eyes   115
The green malignant light of coming storm.
Sir, I was courteous, every phrase well oil'd
As man's could be; yet maiden-meek I pray'd
Concealment: she demanded who we were,
And why we came?   I fabled nothing fair,   120
But, your example pilot, told her all.
Up went the hush'd amaze of hand and eye.
But when I dwelt upon your old affiance,
She answer'd sharply that I talk'd astray.
I urged the fierce inscription on the gate,   125
And our three lives.   True — we had limed ourselves
With open eyes, and we must take the chance.
But such extremes, I told her, well might harm
The woman's cause.   'Not more than now,' she said,
'So puddled as it is with favoritism.'   130
I tried the mother's heart.   Shame might befall
Melissa, knowing, saying not she knew:
Her answer was 'Leave me to deal with that.'
I spoke of war to come and many deaths;
And she replied, her duty was to speak,   135
And duty duty, clear of consequences.
I grew discouraged, Sir; but since I knew
No rock so hard but that a little wave
May beat admission in a thousand years,
I recommenced; 'Decide not ere you pause.   140
I find you here but in the second place,
Some say the third — the authentic foundress you.
I offer boldly: we will seat you highest:
Wink at our advent: help my prince to gain
His rightful bride, and here I promise you   145
Some palace in our land where you shall reign
The head and heart of all our fair she-world,
And your great name flow on with broadening time

For ever.'   Well, she balanced this a little,
And told me she would answer us to-day,   150
Meantime be mute: thus much, nor more I gain'd."

He ceasing, came a message from the Head.
"That afternoon the Princess rode to take
The dip of certain strata to the North.
Would we go with her? we should find the land   155
Worth seeing; and the river made a fall
Out yonder:" then she pointed on to where
A double hill ran up his furrowy forks
Beyond the thick-leaved platans of the vale.

Agreed to this, the day fled on thro' all   160
Its range of duties to the appointed hour.
Then summon'd to the porch we went.   She stood
Among her maidens, higher by the head,
Her back against a pillar, her foot on one
Of those tame leopards.   Kitten-like he roll'd   165
And paw'd about her sandal.   I drew near;
I gazed.   On a sudden my strange seizure came
Upon me, the weird vision of our house:
The Princess Ida seem'd a hollow show,
Her gay-furr'd cats a painted fantasy,   170
Her college and her maidens empty masks,
And I myself the shadow of a dream,
For all things were and were not.   Yet I felt
My heart beat thick with passion and with awe;
Then from my breast the involuntary sigh   175
Brake, as she smote me with the light of eyes
That lent my knee desire to kneel, and shook
My pulses, till to horse we got, and so
Went forth in long retinue following up
The river as it narrow'd to the hills.   180

I rode beside her, and to me she said:
"O friend, we trust that you esteem'd us not
Too harsh to your companion yestermorn;
Unwillingly we spake."   "No — not to her,"
I answer'd, "but to one of whom we spake   185
Your Highness might have seem'd the thing you say."
"Again?" she cried, "are you ambassadresses
From him to me? we give you, being strange,
A license: speak, and let the topic die."

I stammer'd that I knew him — could have wish'd — 190
"Our king expects — was there no precontract?
There is no truer-hearted — ah, you seem
All he prefigured, and he could not see
The bird of passage flying south but long'd
To follow: surely, if your Highness keep   195
Your purport, you will shock him ev'n to death,
Or baser courses, children of despair."

"Poor boy," she said, "can he not read — no books?
Quoit, tennis, ball — no games? nor deals in that
Which men delight in, martial exercise?   200
To nurse a blind ideal like a girl,
Methinks he seems no better than a girl;
As girls were once, as we ourself have been:
We had our dreams; perhaps he mixt with them:
We touch on our dead self, nor shun to do it,   205
Being other — since we learnt our meaning here,
To lift the woman's fall'n divinity
Upon an even pedestal with man."

She paused, and added with a haughtier smile,
"And as to precontracts, we move, my friend,   210
At no man's beck, but know ourself and thee,
O Vashti, noble Vashti!   Summon'd out

She kept her state, and left the drunken king
To brawl at Shushan underneath the palms."

"Alas, your Highness breathes full East," I said,   215
"On that which leans to you.   I know the Prince,
I prize his truth: and then how vast a work
To assail this gray preëminence of man!
You grant me license; might I use it? think;
Ere half be done, perchance your life may fail;   220
Then comes the feebler heiress of your plan,
And takes and ruins all; and thus your pains
May only make that footprint upon sand
Which old-recurring waves of prejudice
Resmooth to nothing: might I dread that you,   225
With only Fame for spouse and your great deeds
For issue, yet may live in vain, and miss,
Meanwhile, what every woman counts her due,
Love, children, happiness?"
                                        And she exclaim'd,
"Peace, you young savage of the Northern wild!   230
What! tho' your Prince's love were like a God's,
Have we not made ourself the sacrifice?
You are bold indeed: we are not talk'd to thus:
Yet will we say for children, would they grew
Like field flowers everywhere! we like them well: 235
But children die; and let me tell you, girl,
Howe'er you babble, great deeds cannot die;
They with the sun and moon renew their light
For ever, blessing those that look on them.
Children — that men may pluck them from our hearts,   240
Kill us with pity, break us with ourselves —
Oh, — children — there is nothing upon earth
More miserable than she that has a son,
And sees him err: nor would we work for fame;
Tho' she perhaps might reap the applause of Great,   245

Who learns the one πον στω whence after-hands
May move the world, tho' she herself effect
But little: wherefore up and act, nor shrink
For fear our solid aim be dissipated
By frail successors.   Would, indeed, we had been,   250
In lieu of many mortal flies, a race
Of giants living, each, a thousand years,
That we might see our own work out, and watch
The sandy footprint harden into stone!"

  I answer'd nothing, doubtful in myself   255
If that strange Poet-princess with her grand
Imaginations might at all be won.
And she broke out, interpreting my thoughts:

  "No doubt we seem a kind of monster to you;
We are used to that: for women, up till this   260
Cramp'd under worse than South-sea-isle taboo,
Dwarfs of the gynæceum, fail so far
In high desire, they know not, cannot guess
How much their welfare is a passion to us.
If we could give them surer, quicker proof —   265
Oh, if our end were less achievable
By slow approaches than by single act
Of immolation, any phase of death,
We were as prompt to spring against the pikes
Or down the fiery gulf as talk of it,   270
To compass our dear sisters' liberties."

  She bow'd as if to veil a noble tear;
And up we came to where the river sloped
To plunge in cataract, shattering on black blocks
A breadth of thunder.   O'er it shook the woods,   275
And danced the color, and, below, stuck out
The bones of some vast bulk that lived and roar'd
Before man was.   She gazed awhile and said,

" As these rude bones to us, are we to her
That will be." " Dare we dream of that," I ask'd,   280
" Which wrought us, as the workman and his work,
That practice betters ? " " How," she cried, " you love
The metaphysics ! read and earn our prize,
A golden brooch : beneath an emerald plane
Sits Diotima, teaching him that died   285
Of hemlock ; our device ; wrought to the life ;
She rapt upon her subject, he on her :
For there are schools for all." " And yet," I said,
" Methinks I have not found among them all
One anatomic." " Nay, we thought of that,"   290
She answer'd, " but it pleased us not : in truth
We shudder but to dream our maids should ape
Those monstrous males that carve the living hound,
And cram him with the fragments of the grave,
Or in the dark dissolving human heart,   295
And holy secrets of this microcosm,
Dabbling a shameless hand with shameful jest,
Encarnalize their spirits : yet we know
Knowledge is knowledge, and this matter hangs :
Howbeit ourself, foreseeing casualty,   300
Nor willing men should come among us, learnt,
For many weary moons before we came,
This craft of healing. Were you sick, ourself
Would tend upon you. To your question now,
Which touches on the workman and his work.   305
Let there be light and there was light : 'tis so :
For was, and is, and will be, are but is ;
And all creation is one act at once,
The birth of light : but we that are not all,
As parts, can see but parts, now this, now that,   310
And live, perforce, from thought to thought, and make
One act a phantom of succession : thus
Our weakness somehow shapes the shadow, Time ;

But in the shadow will we work, and mold
The woman to the fuller day." She spake,   315
With kindled eyes: we rode a league beyond,
And, o'er a bridge of pinewood crossing, came
On flowery levels underneath the crag,
Full of all beauty. "Oh, how sweet," I said
(For I was half-oblivious of my mask),   320
"To linger here with one that loved us." "Yea,"
She answer'd, "or with fair philosophies
That lift the fancy; for indeed these fields
Are lovely, lovelier not the Elysian lawns,
Where paced the Demigods of old, and saw   325
The soft white vapor streak the crownèd towers
Built to the Sun": then, turning to her maids,
"Pitch our pavilion here upon the sward;
Lay out the viands." At the word, they raised
A tent of satin, elaborately wrought   330
With fair Corinna's triumph; here she stood,
Engirt with many a florid maiden-cheek,
The woman-conqueror; woman-conquer'd there
The bearded victor of ten thousand hymns,
And all the men mourn'd at his side: but we   335
Set forth to climb; then, climbing, Cyril kept
With Psyche, with Melissa Florian, I
With mine affianced. Many a little hand
Glanced like a touch of sunshine on the rocks,
Many a light foot shone like a jewel set   340
In the dark crag: and then we turn'd, we wound
About the cliffs, the copses, out and in,
Hammering and clinking, chattering stony names
Of shale and hornblende, rag and trap and tuff,
Amygdaloid and trachyte, till the Sun   345
Grew broader toward his death and fell, and all
The rosy heights came out above the lawns.

The splendor falls on castle walls
  And snowy summits old in story:
The long light shakes across the lakes,
  And the wild cataract leaps in glory.
Blow, bugle, blow; set the wild echoes flying;
Blow, bugle; answer, echoes, dying, dying, dying〉

  Oh hark, oh hear! how thin and clear,
    And thinner, clearer, farther going!
  Oh sweet and far from cliff and scar
    The horns of Elfland faintly blowing!
Blow, let us hear the purple glens replying:
Blow, bugle; answer, echoes, dying, dying, dying!

  O love! they die in yon rich sky,
    They faint on hill or field or river:
  Our echoes roll from soul to soul,
    And grow for ever and for ever.
Blow, bugle, blow; set the wild echoes flying,
And answer, echoes, answer, dying, dying, dying!

Canto IV.

"There sinks the nebulous star we call the Sun,
If that hypothesis of theirs be sound,"
Said Ida; "let us down and rest;" and we
Down from the lean and wrinkled precipices,
By every coppice-feather'd chasm and cleft,   5
Dropt thro' the ambrosial gloom to where below
No bigger than a glowworm shone the tent
Lamp-lit from the inner.   Once she lean'd on me,
Descending; once or twice she lent her hand,
And blissful palpitations in the blood,   10
Stirring a sudden transport, rose and fell.
But when we planted level feet, and dipt
Beneath the satin dome and enter'd in,
There leaning deep in broider'd down we sank
Our elbows: on a tripod in the midst   15

A fragrant flame rose, and before us glow'd
Fruit, blossom, viand, amber wine, and gold.

Then she, " Let some one sing to us: lightlier move
The minutes fledged with music : " and a maid,
Of those beside her, smote her harp, and sang.　　　20

> " Tears, idle tears, I know not what they mean,
> Tears from the depth of some divine despair
> Rise in the heart, and gather to the eyes,
> In looking on the happy Autumn fields,
> And thinking of the days that are no more.　　　25

> " Fresh as the first beam glittering on a sail,
> That brings our friends up from the underworld;
> Sad as the last which reddens over one
> That sinks with all we love below the verge ;
> So sad, so fresh, the days that are no more.　　　30

> "Ah, sad and strange as in dark summer dawns
> The earliest pipe of half-awaken'd birds
> To dying ears, when unto dying eyes
> The casement slowly grows a glimmering square ;
> So sad, so strange, the days that are no more.　　　35

> " Dear as remember'd kisses after death,
> And sweet as those by hopeless fancy feign'd
> On lips that are for others ; deep as love,
> Deep as first love, and wild with all regret ;
> O Death in Life, the days that are no more ! "　　　40

She ended with such passion that the tear,
She sang of, shook and fell, an erring pearl
Lost in her bosom : but with some disdain
Answer'd the Princess, " If indeed there haunt
About the molder'd lodges of the Past　　　45
So sweet a voice and vague, fatal to men,
Well needs it we should cram our ears with wool
And so pace by : but thine are fancies hatch'd

In silken-folded idleness; nor is it
Wiser to weep a true occasion lost,   50
But trim our sails, and let old bygones be,
While down the streams that float us each and all
To the issue, goes, like glittering bergs of ice,
Throne after throne, and, molten on the waste,
Becomes a cloud : for all things serve their time   55
Toward that great year of equal mights and rights,
Nor would I fight with iron laws, in the end
Found golden : let the past be past ; let be
Their cancel'd Babels : tho' the rough kex break
The starr'd mosaic, and the beard-blown goat   60
Hang on the shaft, and the wild fig tree split
Their monstrous idols, care not while we hear
A trumpet in the distance pealing news
Of better, and Hope, a poising eagle, burns
Above the unrisen morrow " : then to me ;   65
" Know you no song of your own land," she said,
" Not such as moans about the retrospect,
But deals with the other distance and the hues
Of promise ; not a death's-head at the wine."

   Then I remember'd one myself had made,   70
What time I watch'd the swallow winging south
From mine own land, part made long since, and part
Now while I sang, and maidenlike as far
As I could ape their treble, did I sing : —

          " O Swallow, Swallow, flying, flying South,   75
       Fly to her, and fall upon her gilded eaves,
       And tell her, tell her, what I tell to thee !

          " Oh tell her, Swallow, thou that knowest each,
       That bright and fierce and fickle is the South,
       And dark and true and tender is the North.   80

"O Swallow, Swallow! if I could follow, and light
Upon her lattice, I would pipe and trill,
And cheep and twitter twenty million loves.

"Oh, were I thou that she might take me in,
And lay me on her bosom, and her heart   85
Would rock the snowy cradle till I died!

"Why lingereth she to clothe her heart with love
Delaying as the tender ash delays
To clothe herself, when all the woods are green?

"Oh tell her, Swallow, that thy brood is flown: 90
Say to her, I do but wanton in the South,
But in the North long since my nest is made.

"Oh tell her, brief is life but love is long,
And brief the sun of summer in the North,
And brief the moon of beauty in the South.   95

"O Swallow, flying from the golden woods,
Fly to her, and pipe and woo her, and make her mine
And tell her, tell her, that I follow thee!"

I ceased, and all the ladies, each at each,
Like the Ithacensian suitors in old time,   100
Stared with great eyes, and laugh'd with alien lips,
And knew not what they meant; for still my voice
Rang false: but smiling, "Not for thee," she said,
"O Bulbul, any rose of Gulistan
Shall burst her veil: marsh-divers, rather, maid,   105
Shall croak thee sister, or the meadow crake
Grate her harsh kindred in the grass: and this
A mere love poem! Oh, for such, my friend,
We hold them slight: they mind us of the time
When we made bricks in Egypt. Knaves are men,   110
That lute and flute fantastic tenderness,
And dress the victim to the offering up.

And paint the gates of Hell with Paradise,
And play the slave to gain the tyranny.
Poor soul! I had a maid of honor once;   115
She wept her true eyes blind for such a one,
A rogue of canzonets and serenades.
I loved her. Peace be with her. She is dead.
So they blaspheme the muse! But great is song
Used to great ends: ourself have often tried   120
Valkyrian hymns, or into rhythm have dash'd
The passion of the prophetess; for song
Is duer unto freedom, force, and growth
Of spirit than to junketing and love.
Love is it? Would this same mock-love, and this   125
Mock-Hymen were laid up like winter bats,
Till all men grew to rate us at our worth,
Not vassals to be beat, nor pretty babes
To be dandled, no, but living wills, and sphered
Whole in ourselves and owed to none! Enough!   130
But now to leaven play with profit, you,
Know you no song, the true growth of your soil,
That gives the manners of your countrywomen?"

     She spoke, and turn'd her sumptuous head with eyes
Of shining expectation fixt on mine.   135
Then while I dragg'd my brains for such a song,
Cyril, with whom the bell-mouth'd glass had wrought,
Or master'd by the sense of sport, began
To troll a careless, careless tavern-catch
Of Moll and Meg, and strange experiences   140
Unmeet for ladies. Florian nodded at him,
I frowning; Psyche flush'd and wann'd and shook;
The lily-like Melissa droop'd her brows;
"Forbear," the Princess cried; "Forbear, Sir," I;
And, heated thro' and thro' with wrath and love,   145
I smote him on the breast; he started up;

There rose a shriek as of a city sack'd;
Melissa clamor'd "Flee the death"; "To horse,"
Said Ida; "home! to horse!" and fled, as flies
A troop of snowy doves athwart the dusk   150
When some one batters at the dovecote doors,
Disorderly the women. Alone I stood
With Florian, cursing Cyril, vext at heart,
In the pavilion: there like parting hopes
I heard them passing from me: hoof by hoof, 155
And every hoof a knell to my desires,
Clang'd on the bridge; and then another shriek,
"The Head, the Head, the Princess, O the Head!"
For blind with rage she miss'd the plank, and roll'd
In the river. Out I sprang from glow to gloom: 160
There whirl'd her white robe like a blossom'd branch
Rapt to the horrible fall: a glance I gave,
No more; but, woman-vested as I was,
Plunged; and the flood drew; yet I caught her; then
Oaring one arm, and bearing in my left 165
The weight of all the hopes of half the world,
Strove to buffet to land in vain. A tree
Was half-disrooted from his place and stoop'd
To drench his dark locks in the gurgling wave
Mid-channel. Right on this we drove and caught, 170
And grasping down the boughs I gain'd the shore.

There stood her maidens glimmeringly group'd
In the hollow bank. One reaching forward drew
My burthen from mine arms; they cried "she lives":
They bore her back into the tent: but I, 175
So much a kind of shame within me wrought,
Not yet endured to meet her opening eyes,
Nor found my friends; but push'd alone on foot
(For since her horse was lost I left her mine)
Across the woods, and less from Indian craft 180

Than beelike instinct hiveward, found at length
The garden portals. Two great statues, Art
And Science, Caryatids, lifted up
A weight of emblem, and betwixt were valves
Of open-work in which the hunter rued   185
His rash intrusion, manlike, but his brows
Had sprouted, and the branches thereupon
Spread out at top, and grimly spiked the gates.

A little space was left between the horns,
Thro' which I clamber'd o'er at top with pain,   190
Dropt on the sward, and up the linden walks,
And, tost on thoughts that changed from hue to hue,
Now poring on the glowworm, now the star,
I paced the terrace, till the Bear had wheel'd
Thro' a great arc his seven slow suns.

                                   A step   195
Of lightest echo, then a loftier form
Than female, moving thro' the uncertain gloom,
Disturb'd me with the doubt "if this were she,"
But it was Florian. "Hist, oh hist!" he said,
"They seek us: out so late is out of rules.   200
Moreover 'seize the strangers' is the cry.
How came you here?" I told him: "I," said he,
"Last of the train, a moral leper, I,
To whom none spake, half-sick at heart, return'd.
Arriving all confused among the rest,   205
With hooded brows I crept into the hall,
And, couch'd behind a Judith, underneath
The head of Holofernes peep'd and saw.
Girl after girl was call'd to trial: each
Disclaim'd all knowledge of us: last of all,   210
Melissa: trust me, Sir, I pitied her.
She, question'd if she knew us men, at first
Was silent; closer prest, denied it not:

And then, demanded if her mother knew,
Or Psyche, she affirm'd not, or denied: 215
From whence the Royal mind, familiar with her,
Easily gather'd either guilt.   She sent
For Psyche, but she was not there; she call'd
For Psyche's child to cast it from the doors;
She sent for Blanche to accuse her face to face;   220
And I slipt out: but whither will you now?
And where are Psyche, Cyril? both are fled:
What, if together? that were not so well.
Would rather we had never come!   I dread
His wildness, and the chances of the dark."   225

"And yet," I said, "you wrong him more than I
That struck him: this is proper to the clown,
Tho' smock'd, or furr'd and purpl'd, still the clown,
To harm the thing that trusts him, and to shame
That which he says he loves: for Cyril, howe'er   230
He deal in frolic, as to-night — the song
Might have been worse, and sinn'd in grosser lips
Beyond all pardon — as it is, I hold
These flashes on the surface are not he.
He has a solid base of temperament: 235
But as the water lily starts and slides
Upon the level in little puffs of wind,
Tho' anchor'd to the bottom, such is he."

Scarce had I ceased when from a tamarisk near
Two proctors leapt upon us, crying, "Names":   240
He, standing still, was clutch'd; but I began
To thrid the musky-circled mazes, wind
And double in and out the boles, and race
By all the fountains: fleet I was of foot:
Before me shower'd the rose in flakes; behind   245
I heard the puff'd pursuer; at mine ear

Bubbled the nightingale and heeded not,
And secret laughter tickled all my soul.
At last I hook'd my ankle in a vine,
That claspt the feet of a Mnemosyne,   250
And falling on my face was caught and known.

They haled us to the Princess where she sat
High in the hall: above her droop'd a lamp,
And made the single jewel on her brow
Burn like the mystic fire on a masthead,   255
Prophet of storm: a handmaid on each side
Bow'd toward her, combing out her long black hair
Damp from the river; and close behind her stood
Eight daughters of the plow, stronger than men,
Huge women blowzed with health, and wind, and rain,   260
And labor. Each was like a Druid rock;
Or like a spire of land that stands apart
Cleft from the main, and wail'd about with mews.

Then, as we came, the crowd dividing clove
An advent to the throne: and therebeside,   265
Half-naked as if caught at once from bed
And tumbled on the purple footcloth, lay
The lily-shining child; and on the left,
Bow'd on her palms and folded up from wrong,
Her round white shoulder shaken with her sobs,   270
Melissa knelt; but Lady Blanche erect
Stood up and spake, an affluent orator.

"It was not thus, O Princess, in old days:
You prized my counsel, lived upon my lips:
I led you then to all the Castalies;   275
I fed you with the milk of every Muse;
I loved you like this kneeler, and you me
Your second mother: those were gracious times.

Then came your new friend: you began to change —
I saw it and grieved — to slacken and to cool;   280
Till, taken with her seeming openness,
You turn'd your warmer currents all to her,
To me you froze: this was my meed for all.
Yet I bore up in part from ancient love,
And partly that I hoped to win you back,   285
And partly conscious of my own deserts,
And partly that you were my civil head,
And chiefly you were born for something great,
In which I might your fellow-worker be,
When time should serve; and thus a noble scheme   290
Grew up from seed we two long since had sown;
In us true growth, in her a Jonah's gourd,
Up in one night and due to sudden sun:
We took this palace; but even from the first
You stood in your own light, and darken'd mine.   295
What student came but that you planed her path
To Lady Psyche, younger, not so wise,
A foreigner, and I your countrywoman,
I your old friend and tried, she new in all?
But still her lists were swell'd, and mine were lean;   300
Yet I bore up in hope she would be known:
Then came these wolves: *they* knew her: *they* endured,
Long-closeted with her the yestermorn,
To tell her what they were, and she to hear:
And me none told: not less to an eye like mine,   305
A lidless watcher of the public weal,
Last night, their mask was patent, and my foot
Was to you: but I thought again: I fear'd
To meet a cold ' We thank you, we shall hear of it
From Lady Psyche ': you had gone to her,   310
She told, perforce; and winning easy grace,
No doubt, for slight delay, remain'd among us
In our young nursery still unknown, the stem

Less grain than touchwood, while my honest heat
Were all miscounted as malignant haste   315
To push my rival out of place and power.
But public use required she should be known;
And since my oath was ta'en for public use,
I broke the letter of it to keep the sense.
I spoke not then at first, but watch'd them well,   320
Saw that they kept apart, no mischief done;
And yet this day (tho' you should hate me for it)
I came to tell you; found that you had gone,
Ridd'n to the hills, she likewise: now, I thought,
That surely she will speak; if not, then I.   325
Did she?   These monsters blazon'd what they were,
According to the coarseness of their kind,
For thus I hear; and known at last (my work),
And full of cowardice and guilty shame,
I grant in her some sense of shame, she flies;   330
And I remain on whom to wreak your rage,
I, that have lent my life to build up yours,
I that have wasted here health, wealth, and time,
And talent, I — you know it — I will not boast:
Dismiss me, and I prophesy your plan,   335
Divorced from my experience, will be chaff
For every gust of chance, and men will say
We did not know the real light, but chased
The wisp that flickers where no foot can tread."

     She ceased: the Princess answer'd coldly, " Good: 340
Your oath is broken: we dismiss you: go.
For this lost lamb (she pointed to the child),
Our mind is changed: we take it to ourself."

     Thereat the Lady stretch'd a vulture throat,
And shot from crooked lips a haggard smile.   345
"The plan was mine.   I built the nest," she said,

"To hatch the cuckoo.   Rise!" and stoop'd to updrag
Melissa: she, half on her mother propt,
Half-drooping from her, turn'd her face, and cast
A liquid look on Ida, full of prayer   350
Which melted Florian's fancy as she hung,
A Niobëan daughter, one arm out,
Appealing to the bolts of Heaven; and while
We gazed upon her came a little stir
About the doors, and on a sudden rush'd   355
Among us, out of breath, as one pursued,
A woman-post in flying raiment.   Fear
Stared in her eyes, and chalk'd her face, and wing'd
Her transit to the throne, whereby she fell
Delivering seal'd dispatches which the Head   360
Took half-amazed, and in her lion's mood
Tore open, silent we with blind surmise
Regarding, while she read, till over brow
And cheek and bosom brake the wrathful bloom,
As of some fire against a stormy cloud   365
When the wild peasant rights himself, the rick
Flames, and his anger reddens in the heavens;
For anger most it seem'd, while now her breast,
Beaten with some great passion at her heart,
Palpitated, her hand shook, and we heard   370
In the dead hush the papers that she held
Rustle: at once the lost lamb at her feet
Sent out a bitter bleating for its dam;
The plaintive cry jarr'd on her ire; she crush'd
The scrolls together, made a sudden turn   375
As if to speak, but, utterance failing her,
She whirl'd them on to me, as who should say
"Read," and I read — two letters — one her sire's.

    "Fair daughter, when we sent the Prince your way
We knew not your ungracious laws, which learnt,   380

We, conscious of what temper you are built,
Came all in haste to hinder wrong, but fell
Into his father's hands, who has this night,
You lying close upon his territory,
Slipt round and in the dark invested you,   385
And here he keeps me hostage for his son."

The second was my father's, running thus:
" You have our son: touch not a hair of his head:
Render him up unscathed: give him your hand:
Cleave to your contract: tho' indeed we hear   390
You hold the woman is the better man;
A rampant heresy, such as if it spread
Would make all women kick against their Lords
Thro' all the world, and which might well deserve
That we this night should pluck your palace down; 395
And we will do it, unless you send us back
Our son, on the instant, whole."
                   So far I read;
And then stood up and spoke impetuously.

" Oh, not to pry and peer on your reserve,
But led by golden wishes and a hope,   400
The child of regal compact, did I break
Your precinct; not a scorner of your sex,
But venerator, zealous it should be
All that it might be: hear me, for I bear,
Tho' man, yet human, whatsoe'er your wrongs,   405
From the flaxen curl to the gray lock a life
Less mine than yours: my nurse would tell me of you;
I babbled for you, as babies for the moon,
Vague brightness; when a boy, you stoop'd to me
From all high places, lived in all fair lights, 410
Came in long breezes rapt from inmost South
And blown to inmost North; at eve and dawn

With Ida, Ida, Ida rang the woods;
The leader wildswan in among the stars
Would clang it, and, lapt in wreaths of glowworm light,　415
The mellow breaker murmur'd Ida.　Now,
Because I would have reach'd you, had you been
Sphered up with Cassiopëia, or the enthroned
Persephonè in Hades, now at length,
Those winters of abeyance all worn out,　　　　　　　420
A man I came to see you: but, indeed,
Not in this frequence can I lend full tongue,
O noble Ida, to those thoughts that wait
On you, their center: let me say but this,
That many a famous man and woman, town　　　　　425
And landskip, have I heard of, after seen
The dwarfs of presage: tho' when known, there grew
Another kind of beauty in detail
Made them worth knowing; but in you I found
My boyish dream involved and dazzled down　　　　430
And master'd, while that after-beauty makes
Such head from act to act, from hour to hour,
Within me, that except you slay me here,
According to your bitter statute book,
I cannot cease to follow you, as they say　　　　　435
The seal does music; who desire you more
Than growing boys their manhood; dying lips,
With many thousand matters left to do,
The breath of life; oh, more than poor men wealth,
Than sick men health — yours, yours, not mine — but half
Without you; with you, whole; and of those halves,　441
You worthiest; and howe'er you block and bar
Your heart with system out from mine, I hold
That it becomes no man to nurse despair,
But in the teeth of clench'd antagonisms　　　　　445
To follow up the worthiest till he die:
Yet that I came not all unauthorized

Behold your father's letter."
                                    On one knee
Kneeling, I gave it, which she caught, and dash'd
Unopen'd at her feet: a tide of fierce   450
Invective seem'd to wait behind her lips,
As waits a river level with the dam
Ready to burst and flood the world with foam:
And so she would have spoken, but there rose
A hubbub in the court of half the maids   455
Gather'd together: from the illumined hall
Long lanes of splendor slanted o'er a press
Of snowy shoulders, thick as herded ewes.
And rainbow robes, and gems and gemlike eyes,
And gold and golden heads; they to and fro   460
Fluctuated, as flowers in storm, some red, some pale,
All open-mouth'd, all gazing to the light,
Some crying there was an army in the land,
And some that men were in the very walls,
And some they cared not; till a clamor grew   465
As of a new-world Babel, woman-built
And worse-confounded: high above them stood
The placid marble Muses, looking peace.

Not peace she look'd, the Head: but, rising up
Robed in the long night of her deep hair, so   470
To the open window moved, remaining there
Fixt like a beacon tower above the waves
Of tempest, when the crimson-rolling eye
Glares ruin, and the wild birds on the light
Dash themselves dead. She stretch'd her arms and call'd
Across the tumult, and the tumult fell.   476

   "What fear ye, brawlers? am not I your Head?
On me, me, me, the storm first breaks: *I* dare
All these male thunderbolts: what is it ye fear?

Peace! there are those to avenge us, and they come: 480
If not, — myself were like enough, O girls,
To unfurl the maiden banner of our rights,
And, clad in iron, burst the ranks of war,
Or, falling, protomartyr of our cause,
Die: yet I blame you not so much for fear;   485
Six thousand years of fear have made you that
From which I would redeem you: but for those
That stir this hubbub — you and you — I know
Your faces there in the crowd — to-morrow morn
We hold a great convention: then shall they   490
That love their voices more than duty learn
With whom they deal, dismiss'd in shame to live
No wiser than their mothers, household staff,
Live chattels, mincers of each other's fame,
Full of weak poison, turnspits for the clown,   495
The drunkard's football, laughing-stocks of Time,
Whose brains are in their hands and in their heels,
But fit to flaunt, to dress, to dance, to thrum,
To tramp, to scream, to burnish, and to scour,
For ever slaves at home and fools abroad."   500

She, ending, waved her hands: thereat the crowd
Muttering, dissolved: then with a smile, that look'd
A stroke of cruel sunshine on the cliff,
When all the glens are drown'd in azure gloom
Of thunder shower, she floated to us and said: 505

"You have done well and like a gentleman,
And like a prince: you have our thanks for all:
And you look well too in your woman's dress:
Well have you done and like a gentleman.
You saved our life: we owe you bitter thanks: 510
Better have died and spilt our bones in the flood —
Then men had said — but now — What hinders me
To take such bloody vengeance on you both? —

Yet since our father — Wasps in our good hive,
You would-be quenchers of the light to be, 515
Barbarians, grosser than your native bears —
Oh would I had his scepter for one hour!
You that have dared to break our bound, and gull'd
Our servants, wrong'd and lied and thwarted us —
I wed with thee! *I* bound by precontract 520
Your bride, your bondslave! not tho' all the gold
That veins the world were pack'd to make your crown,
And every spoken tongue should lord you. Sir,
Your falsehood and yourself are hateful to us:
I trample on your offers and on you: 525
Begone: we will not look upon you more.
Here, push them out at gates."
                    In wrath she spake.
Then those eight mighty daughters of the plow
Bent their broad faces toward us and address'd
Their motion: twice I sought to plead my cause, 530
But on my shoulder hung their heavy hands,
The weight of destiny: so from her face
They push'd us, down the steps, and thro' the court,
And with grim laughter thrust us out at gates.

We cross'd the street and gain'd a petty mound 535
Beyond it, whence we saw the lights and heard
The voices murmuring. While I listen'd, came
On a sudden the weird seizure and the doubt:
I seem'd to move among a world of ghosts;
The Princess with her monstrous woman-guard, 540
The jest and earnest working side by side,
The cataract and the tumult and the kings
Were shadows; and the long fantastic night
With all its doings had and had not been,
And all things were and were not.
                    This went by 545

As strangely as it came, and on my spirits
Settled a gentle cloud of melancholy;
Not long; I shook it off; for spite of doubts
And sudden ghostly shadowings I was one
To whom the touch of all mischance but came   550
As night to him that sitting on a hill
Sees the midsummer, midnight, Norway sun
Set into sunrise; then we moved away.

> Thy voice is heard thro' rolling drums,
>   That beat to battle where he stands;   555
> Thy face across his fancy comes,
>   And gives the battle to his hands:
> A moment, while the trumpets blow,
>   He sees his brood about thy knee;
> The next, like fire he meets the foe,   560
>   And strikes him dead for thine and thee.

So Lilia sang: we thought her half-possess'd,
She struck such warbling fury thro' the words;
And, after, feigning pique at what she call'd
The raillery, or grotesque, or false sublime —   565
Like one that wishes at a dance to change
The music — clapt her hands and cried for war,
Or some grand fight to kill and make an end:
And he that next inherited the tale,
Half turning to the broken statue, said,   570
"Sir Ralph has got your colors: if I prove
Your knight, and fight your battle, what for me?"
It chanced, her empty glove upon the tomb
Lay by her like a model of her hand.
She took it and she flung it. "Fight," she said,   575
"And make us all we would be, great and good."
He, knightlike in his cap instead of casque,
A cap of Tyrol borrow'd from the hall,
Arranged the favor, and assumed the Prince.

Canto V.

Now, scarce three paces measured from the mound,
We stumbled on a stationary voice,
And "Stand, who goes?" "Two from the palace," I.
"The second two: they wait," he said, "pass on;
His Highness wakes": and one, that clash'd in arms,   5
By glimmering lanes and walls of canvas led,
Threading the soldier-city, till we heard
The drowsy folds of our great ensign shake
From blazon'd lions o'er the imperial tent
Whispers of war.

            Entering, the sudden light   10
Dazed me half-blind: I stood and seem'd to hear,
As in a poplar grove when a light wind wakes
A lisping of the innumerous leaf and dies,
Each hissing in his neighbor's ear; and then
A strangled titter, out of which there brake   15
On all sides, clamoring etiquette to death,
Unmeasured mirth; while now the two old kings
Began to wag their baldness up and down,
The fresh young captains flash'd their glittering teeth,
The huge bush-bearded Barons heaved and blew,   20
And, slain with laughter, roll'd the gilded Squire.

At length my Sire, his rough cheek wet with tears,
Panted, from weary sides, "King, you are free!
We did but keep you surety for our son,
If this be he,—or a draggled mawkin, thou,   25
That tends her bristled grunters in the sludge:"
For I was drench'd with ooze, and torn with briers,
More crumpled than a poppy from the sheath,
And all one rag, disprinced from head to heel.
Then some one sent beneath his vaulted palm   30

A whisper'd jest to some one near him, " Look,
He has been among his shadows."   " Satan take
The old women and their shadows! (thus the King
Roar'd).   Make yourself a man to fight with men.
Go: Cyril told us all."

     As boys that slink 35
From ferule and the trespass-chiding eye,
Away we stole, and transient in a trice
From what was left of faded woman-slough
To sheathing splendors and the golden scale
Of harness, issued in the sun, that now 40
Leapt from the dewy shoulders of the Earth,
And hit the Northern hills.   Here Cyril met us.
A little shy at first, but by and by
We twain, with mutual pardon ask'd and given
For stroke and song, resolder'd peace, whereon 45
Follow'd his tale.   Amazed he fled away
Thro' the dark land, and later in the night
Had come on Psyche weeping: "then we fell
Into your father's hand, and there she lies,
But will not speak, nor stir."

     He show'd a tent 50
A stone-shot off: we enter'd in, and there
Among piled arms and rough accouterments,
Pitiful sight, wrapp'd in a soldier's cloak,
Like some sweet sculpture draped from head to foot,
And push'd by rude hands from its pedestal, 55
All her fair length upon the ground she lay:
And at her head a follower of the camp,
A charr'd and wrinkled piece of womanhood,
Sat watching like a watcher by the dead.

 Then Florian knelt, and " Come " he whisper'd to her, 60
" Lift up your head, sweet sister: lie not thus.
What have you done but right? you could not slay

Me, nor your prince: look up: be comforted:
Sweet is it to have done the thing one ought,
When fall'n in darker ways."   And likewise I: 65
"Be comforted: have I not lost her too,
In whose least act abides the nameless charm
That none has else for me?"   She heard, she moved,
She moan'd, a folded voice; and up she sat,
And raised the cloak from brows as pale and smooth   70
As those that mourn half-shrouded over death
In deathless marble.   "Her," she said, "my friend —
Parted from her — betray'd her cause and mine —
Where shall I breathe? why kept ye not your faith?
Oh, base and bad! what comfort? none for me!"   75
To whom remorseful Cyril, "Yet I pray
Take comfort: live, dear lady, for your child!"
At which she lifted up her voice and cried.

"Ah me, my babe, my blossom, ah, my child,
My one sweet child, whom I shall see no more!   80
For now will cruel Ida keep her back;
And either she will die from want of care,
Or sicken with ill-usage, when they say
The child is hers — for every little fault,
The child is hers; and they will beat my girl   85
Remembering her mother: O my flower!
Or they will take her, they will make her hard,
And she will pass me by in after-life
With some cold reverence worse than were she dead.
Ill mother that I was to leave her there,   90
To lag behind, scared by the cry they made,
The horror of the shame among them all:
But I will go and sit beside the doors,
And make a wild petition night and day,
Until they hate to hear me like a wind   95
Wailing for ever, till they open to me,

And lay my little blossom at my feet,
My babe, my sweet Aglaia, my one child:
And I will take her up and go my way,
And satisfy my soul with kissing her: **100**
Ah! what might that man not deserve of me
Who gave me back my child?"   "Be comforted,"
Said Cyril, "you shall have it": but again
She veil'd her brows, and prone she sank, and so
Like tender things that being caught feign death,
Spoke not, nor stirr'd.   **105**
           By this a murmur ran
Thro' all the camp, and inward raced the scouts
With rumor of Prince Arac hard at hand.
We left her by the woman, and without
Found the gray kings at parle: and, "Look you," cried   **110**
My father, "that our compact be fulfill'd:
You have spoilt this child; she laughs at you and man:
She wrongs herself, her sex, and me, and him:
But red-faced war has rods of steel and fire;
She yields, or war."
           Then Gama turn'd to me: **115**
"We fear, indeed, you spent a stormy time
With our strange girl; and yet they say that still
You love her.   Give us, then, your mind at large:
How say you, war or not?"
           "Not war, if possible,
O king," I said, "lest from the abuse of war,   **120**
The desecrated shrine, the trampled year,
The smoldering homestead, and the household flower
Torn from the lintel — all the common wrong —
A smoke go up thro' which I loom to her
Three times a monster: now she lightens scorn   **125**
At him that mars her plan, but then would hate
(And every voice she talk'd with ratify it,
And every face she look'd on justify it)

The general foe. More soluble is this knot,
By gentleness than war. I want her love.   130
What were I nigher this altho' we dash'd
Your cities into shards with catapults,
She would not love; — or brought her chain'd, a slave,
The lifting of whose eyelash is my lord,
Not ever would she love; but, brooding, turn   ·135
The book of scorn till all my flitting chance
Were caught within the record of her wrongs,
And crush'd to death : and rather, Sire, than this
I would the old God of war himself were dead,
Forgotten, rusting on his iron hills,   140
Rotting on some wild shore with ribs of wreck,
Or like an old-world mammoth bulk'd in ice,
Not to be molten out."
                                    And roughly spake
My father, " Tut, you know them not, the girls.
Boy, when I hear you prate I almost think   145
That idiot legend credible.   Look you, Sir !
Man is the hunter; woman is his game:
The sleek and shining creatures of the chase,
We hunt them for the beauty of their skins;
They love us for it, and we ride them down.   150
Wheedling and siding with them !   Out! for shame !
Boy, there's no rose that's half so dear to them
As he that does the thing they dare not do,
Breathing and sounding beauteous battle, comes
With the air of the trumpet round him, and leaps in   155
Among the women, snares them by the score
Flatter'd and fluster'd, wins, tho' dash'd with death
He reddens what he kisses: thus I won
Your mother, a good mother, a good wife,
Worth winning; but this firebrand — gentleness   160
To such as her! if Cyril spake her true,
To catch a dragon in a cherry net,

To trip a tigress with a gossamer,
Were wisdom to it."
                    " Yea, but Sire," I cried,
" Wild natures need wise curbs. The soldier ? No: 165
What dares not Ida do that she should prize
The soldier ?   I beheld her, when she rose
The yesternight, and storming in extremes,
Stood for her cause, and flung defiance down
Gagelike to man, and had not shunn'd the death,   170
No, not the soldier's: yet I hold her, king,
True woman: but you clash them all in one,
That have as many differences as we.
The violet varies from the lily as far
As oak from elm: one loves the soldier, one   175
The silken priest of peace, one this, one that,
And some unworthily; their sinless faith,
A maiden moon that sparkles on a sty,
Glorifying clown and satyr; whence they need
More breadth of culture: is not Ida right?   180
They worth it ? truer to the law within ?
Severer in the logic of a life ?
Twice as magnetic to sweet influences
Of earth and heaven ? and she of whom you speak,
My mother, looks as whole as some serene   185
Creation minted in the golden moods
Of sovereign artists; not a thought, a touch,
But pure as lines of green that streak the white
Of the first snowdrop's inner leaves; I say,
Not like the piebald miscellany, man,   190
Bursts of great heart and slips in sensual mire,
But whole and one: and, take them all-in-all,
Were we ourselves but half as good, as kind,
As truthful, much that Ida claims as right
Had ne'er been mooted, but as frankly theirs   195
As dues of Nature.   To our point: not war:

Lest I lose all."
                  "Nay, nay, you spake but sense,"
Said Gama. "We remember love ourself
In our sweet youth; we did not rate him then
This red-hot iron to be shaped with blows. 200
You talk almost like Ida: *she* can talk;
And there is something in it as you say:
But you talk kindlier: we esteem you for it. —
He seems a gracious and a gallant Prince,
I would he had our daughter: for the rest, 205
Our own detention, why, the causes weigh'd,
Fatherly fears — you used us courteously —
We would do much to gratify your Prince —
We pardon it; and for your ingress here
Upon the skirt and fringe of our fair land, 210
You did but come as goblins in the night,
Nor in the furrow broke the plowman's head,
Nor burnt the grange, nor buss'd the milking-maid,
Nor robb'd the farmer of his bowl of cream:
But let your Prince (our royal word upon it, 215
He comes back safe) ride with us to our lines,
And speak with Arac: Arac's word is thrice
As ours with Ida: something may be done —
I know not what — and ours shall see us friends.
You, likewise, our late guests, if so you will, 220
Follow us: who knows? we four may build some plan
Foursquare to opposition."
                  Here he reach'd
White hands of farewell to my sire, who growl'd
An answer which, half-muffled in his beard,
Let so much out as gave us leave to go. 225

Then rode we with the old king across the lawns
Beneath huge trees, a thousand rings of Spring
In every bole, a song on every spray

Of birds that piped their Valentines, and woke
Desire in me to infuse my tale of love   230
In the old king's ears, who promised help, and oozed
All o'er with honey'd answer as we rode,
And blossom-fragrant slipt the heavy dews
Gather'd by night and peace, with each light air
On our mail'd heads: but other thoughts than peace   235
Burnt in us when we saw the embattled squares,
And squadrons of the Prince trampling the flowers
With clamor: for among them rose a cry
As if to greet the king; they made a halt;
The horses yell'd; they clash'd their arms; the drum   240
Beat; merrily-blowing shrill'd the martial fife;
And in the blast and bray of the long horn
And serpent-throated bugle, undulated
The banner: anon to meet us lightly pranced
Three captains out; nor ever had I seen   245
Such thews of men: the midmost and the highest
Was Arac: all about his motion clung
The shadow of his sister, as the beam
Of the East, that play'd upon them, made them glance
Like those three stars of the airy Giant's zone,   250
That glitter burnish'd by the frosty dark;
And as the fiery Sirius alters hue,
And bickers into red and emerald, shone
Their morions, wash'd with morning, as they came.

  And I that prated peace, when first I heard   255
War-music, felt the blind wildbeast of force,
Whose home is in the sinews of a man,
Stir in me as to strike: then took the king
His three broad sons; with now a wandering hand,
And now a pointed finger, told them all: 260
A common light of smiles at our disguise
Broke from their lips, and, ere the windy jest

Had labor'd down within his ample lungs,
The genial giant, Arac, roll'd himself
Thrice in the saddle, then burst out in words.   265

"Our land invaded, 's death! and he himself
Your captive, yet my father wills not war:
And, 's death! myself, what care I, war or no?
But then this question of your troth remains:
And there's a downright honest meaning in her;   270
She flies too high, she flies too high! and yet
She ask'd but space and fairplay for her scheme;
She prest and prest it on me — I myself,
What know I of these things? but, life and soul!
I thought her half-right talking of her wrongs;   275
I say she flies too high, 's death! what of that?
I take her for the flower of womankind,
And so I often told her, right or wrong,
And, Prince, she can be sweet to those she loves,
And, right or wrong, I care not: this is all,   280
I stand upon her side: she made me swear it —
'S death — and with solemn rites by candle-light —
Swear by St. something — I forget her name —
Her that talk'd down the fifty wisest men;
She was a princess too; and so I swore.   285
Come, this is all; she will not: waive your claim:
If not, the foughten field, what else, at once
Decides it, 's death! against my father's will."

I lagg'd in answer, loth to render up
My precontract, and loth by brainless war   290
To cleave the rift of difference deeper yet;
Till one of those two brothers, half aside
And fingering at the hair about his lip,
To prick us on to combat, " Like to like!
The woman's garment hid the woman's heart."   295

A taunt that clench'd his purpose like a blow!
For fiery-short was Cyril's counter-scoff,
And sharp I answer'd, touch'd upon the point
Where idle boys are cowards to their shame,
"Decide it here: why not? we are three to three."   300

   Then spake the third, "But three to three? no more?
No more, and in our noble sister's cause?
More, more, for honor: every captain waits
Hungry for honor, angry for his king.
More, more, some fifty on a side, that each   305
May breathe himself, and quick! by overthrow
Of these or those, the question settled die."
" Yea," answer'd I, " for this wild wreath of air,
This flake of rainbow flying on the highest
Foam of men's deeds — this honor, if ye will.   310
It needs must be for honor if at all:
Since, what decision? if we fail, we fail,
And if we win, we fail: she would not keep
Her compact."   "'S death! but we will send to her,"
Said Arac, "worthy reasons why she should   315
Bide by this issue: let our missive thro',
And you shall have her answer by the word."

   "Boys!" shriek'd the old king, but vainlier than a hen
To her false daughters in the pool; for none
Regarded; neither seem'd there more to say: 320
Back rode we to my father's camp, and found
He thrice had sent a herald to the gates,
To learn if Ida yet would cede our claim,
Or by denial flush her babbling wells
With her own people's life: three times he went: 325
The first, he blew and blew, but none appear'd:
He batter'd at the doors; none came: the next,
An awful voice within had warn'd him thence:

The third, and those eight daughters of the plow
Came sallying thro' the gates, and caught his hair,   330
And so belabor'd him on rib and cheek
They made him wild: not less one glance he caught
Thro' open doors of Ida station'd there
Unshaken, clinging to her purpose, firm
Tho' compass'd by two armies and the noise   335
Of arms; and standing like a stately pine
Set in a cataract on an island-crag,
When storm is on the heights, and right and left
Suck'd from the dark heart of the long hills roll
The torrents, dash'd to the vale: and yet her will   340
Bred will in me to overcome it or fall.

   But when I told the king that I was pledged
To fight in tourney for my bride, he clash'd
His iron palms together with a cry;
Himself would tilt it out among the lads: 345
But overborne by all his bearded lords
With reasons drawn from age and state, perforce
He yielded, wroth and red, with fierce demur:
And many a bold knight started up in heat,
And sware to combat for my claim till death.   350

   All on this side the palace ran the field
Flat to the garden-wall: and likewise here,
Above the garden's glowing blossom-belts,
A column'd entry shone and marble stairs,
And great bronze valves, emboss'd with Tomyris   355
And what she did to Cyrus after fight,
But now fast barr'd: so here upon the flat
All that long morn the lists were hammer'd up,
And all that morn the heralds to and fro,
With message and defiance, went and came;   360
Last, Ida's answer, in a royal hand,

But shaken here and there, and rolling words
Oration-like.   I kiss'd it and I read.

    " O brother, you have known the pangs we felt,
What heats of indignation when we heard   365
Of those that iron-cramp'd their women's feet;
Of lands in which at the altar the poor bride
Gives her harsh groom for bridal-gift a scourge;
Of living hearts that crack within the fire
Where smolder their dead despots; and of those, —   370
Mothers, — that, all prophetic pity, fling
Their pretty maids in the running flood, and swoops
The vulture, beak and talon, at the heart
Made for all noble motion: and I saw
That equal baseness lived in sleeker times   375
With smoother men: the old leaven leaven'd all:
Millions of throats would bawl for civil rights,
No woman named: therefore I set my face
Against all men, and lived but for mine own.
Far off from men I built a fold for them: 380
I stored it full of rich memorial:
I fenced it round with gallant institutes,
And biting laws to scare the beasts of prey;
And prosper'd till a rout of saucy boys
Brake on us at our books, and marr'd our peace,   385
Mask'd like our maids, blustering I know not what
Of insolence and love, some pretext held
Of baby troth, invalid, since my will
Seal'd not the bond — the striplings! — for their sport! —
I tamed my leopards: shall I not tame these?   390
Or you? or I? for since you think me touch'd
In honor — what, I would not aught of false —
Is not our cause pure?   And whereas I know
Your prowess, Arac, and what mother's blood
You draw from, fight; you failing, I abide   395

What end soever: fail you will not.   Still
Take not his life: he risk'd it for my own;
His mother lives: yet whatsoe'er you do,
Fight, and fight well; strike, and strike home.   O dear
Brothers! the woman's Angel guards you, you   400
The sole men to be mingled with our cause,
The sole men we shall prize in the aftertime,
Your very armor hallow'd, and your statues
Rear'd, sung to, when, this gadfly brush'd aside,
We plant a solid foot into the Time,   405
And mold a generation strong to move
With claim on claim from right to right, till she
Whose name is yoked with children's, know herself;
And Knowledge in our own land make her free,
And, ever following those two crownèd twins,   410
Commerce and conquest, shower the fiery grain
Of freedom broadcast over all that orbs
Between the Northern and the Southern morn."

Then came a postscript dash'd across the rest.
" See that there be no traitors in your camp: 415
We seem a nest of traitors — none to trust
Since our arms fail'd — this Egypt-plague of men!
Almost our maids were better at their homes,
Than thus man-girdled here: indeed I think
Our chiefest comfort is the little child   420
Of one unworthy mother; which she left:
She shall not have it back: the child shall grow
To prize the authentic mother of her mind.
I took it for an hour in mine own bed
This morning: there the tender orphan hands   425
Felt at my heart, and seem'd to charm from thence
The wrath I nursed against the world: farewell."

I ceased; he said, " Stubborn, but she may sit
Upon a king's right hand in thunderstorms,

And breed up warriors !　See now, tho' yourself　　　　430
Be dazzled by the wildfire Love to sloughs
That swallow common sense, the spindling king,
This Gama swamp'd in lazy tolerance.
When the man wants weight, the woman takes it up,
And topples down the scales ; but this is fixt　　　　435
As are the roots of earth and base of all ;
Man for the field, and woman for the hearth :
Man for the sword, and for the needle she :
Man with the head, and woman with the heart :
Man to command, and woman to obey ;　　　　440
All else confusion.　Look you ! the gray mare
Is ill to live with, when her whinny shrills
From tile to scullery, and her small goodman
Shrinks in his arm-chair while the fires of Hell
Mix with his hearth : but you — she's yet a colt —　　　445
Take, break her : strongly groom'd and straitly curb'd
She might not rank with those detestable
That let the bantling scald at home, and brawl
Their rights or wrongs like potherbs in the street.
They say she's comely ; there's the fairer chance :　　　450
I like her none the less for rating at her !
Besides, the woman wed is not as we,
But suffers change of frame.　A lusty brace
Of twins may weed her of her folly.　Boy,
The bearing and the training of a child　　　　455
Is woman's wisdom."
　　　　　　　　Thus the hard old king :
I took my leave, for it was nearly noon :
I pored upon her letter which I held,
And on the little clause "take not his life" :
I mused on that wild morning in the woods,　　　　460
And on the " Follow, follow, thou shalt win " :
I thought on all the wrathful king had said,
And how the strange betrothment was to end :

Then I remember'd that burnt sorcerer's curse —
That one should fight with shadows, and should fall;   465
And like a flash the weird affection came:
King, camp, and college turn'd to hollow shows;
I seem'd to move in old memorial tilts,
And doing battle with forgotten ghosts,
To dream myself the shadow of a dream: 470
And ere I woke it was the point of noon,
The lists were ready. Empanoplied and plumed,
We enter'd in and waited, fifty there
Opposed to fifty, till the trumpet blared
At the barrier like a wild horn in a land   475
Of echoes, and a moment, and once more
The trumpet, and again: at which the storm
Of galloping hoofs bare on the ridge of spears
And riders front to front, until they closed
In conflict with the crash of shivering points,   480
And thunder. Yet it seem'd a dream, I dream'd
Of fighting. On his haunches rose the steed,
And into fiery splinters leapt the lance,
And out of stricken helmets sprang the fire.
Part sat like rocks: part reel'd but kept their seats: 485
Part roll'd on the earth, and rose again and drew:
Part stumbled mixt with floundering horses. Down
From those two bulks at Arac's side, and down
From Arac's arm, as from a giant's flail,
The large blows rain'd, as here and everywhere   490
He rode the mellay, lord of the ringing lists
And all the plain, — brand, mace, and shaft, and shield —
Shock'd, like an iron-clanging anvil bang'd
With hammers; till I thought, can this be he
From Gama's dwarfish loins? If this be so,   495
The mother makes us most — and in my dream
I glanced aside, and saw the palace-front
Alive with fluttering scarfs and ladies' eyes,

And highest, among the statues, statue-like,
Between a cymbal'd Miriam and a Jael,   500
With Psyche's babe, was Ida watching us,
A single band of gold about her hair,
Like a Saint's glory up in heaven: but she
No saint — inexorable — no tenderness —
Too hard, too cruel: yet she sees me fight,   505
Yea, let her see me fall!   With that I drave
Among the thickest and bore down a prince,
And Cyril, one.   Yea, let me make my dream
All that I would.   But that large-molded man,
His visage all agrin as at a wake,   510
Made at me thro' the press, and, staggering back
With stroke on stroke the horse and horseman, came
As comes a pillar of electric cloud,
Flaying the roofs and sucking up the drains,
And shadowing down the champaign till it strikes   515
On a wood, and takes, and breaks, and cracks, and splits,
And twists the grain with such a roar that Earth
Reels, and the herdsmen cry; for everything
Gave way before him: only Florian, he
That loved me closer than his own right eye,   520
Thrust in between; but Arac rode him down:
And Cyril seeing it, push'd against the Prince,
With Psyche's color round his helmet, tough,
Strong, supple, sinew-corded, apt at arms;
But tougher, heavier, stronger, he that smote   525
And threw him: last I spurr'd; I felt my veins
Stretch with fierce heat; a moment hand to hand,
And sword to sword, and horse to horse we hung,
Till I struck out and shouted; the blade glanced,
I did but shear a feather, and dream and truth   530
Flow'd from me; darkness closed me; and I fell.

Home they brought her warrior dead:
    She nor swoon'd, nor utter'd cry:
All her maidens, watching, said,
    "She must weep or she will die."

Then they praised him, soft and low,
    Call'd him worthy to be loved,
Truest friend and noblest foe;
    Yet she neither spoke nor moved.

Stole a maiden from her place,
    Lightly to the warrior stept,
Took the face-cloth from the face;
    Yet she neither moved nor wept.

Rose a nurse of ninety years,
    Set his child upon her knee —
Like summer tempest came her tears —
    "Sweet my child, I live for thee."

———————

Canto VI.

My dream had never died or lived again.
As in some mystic middle state I lay;
Seeing I saw not, hearing not I heard:
Tho', if I saw not, yet they told me all
So often that I speak as having seen.   5
For so it seem'd, or so they said to me,
That all things grew more tragic and more strange;
That when our side was vanquish'd, and my cause
For ever lost, there went up a great cry,
The Prince is slain.   My father heard and ran   10
In on the lists, and there unlaced my casque
And grovel'd on my body, and after him
Came Psyche, sorrowing for Aglaia.

    But high upon the palace Ida stood
With Psyche's babe in arm: there on the roofs   15
Like that great dame of Lapidoth she sang.

"Our enemies have fall'n, have fall'n : the seed,
The little seed they laugh'd at in the dark,
Has risen and cleft the soil, and grown a bulk
Of spanless girth, that lays on every side   20
A thousand arms and rushes to the Sun.

"Our enemies have fall'n, have fall'n : they came ;
The leaves were wet with women's tears : they heard
A noise of songs they would not understand :
They mark'd it with the red cross to the fall,   25
And would have strown it, and are fall'n themselves.

"Our enemies have fall'n, have fall'n : they came,
The woodmen with their axes : lo the tree !
But we will make it fagots for the hearth,
And shape it plank and beam for roof and floor,   30
And boats and bridges for the use of men.

"Our enemies have fall'n, have fall'n : they struck ;
With their own blows they hurt themselves, nor knew
There dwelt an iron nature in the grain :
The glittering ax was broken in their arms,   35
Their arms were shatter'd to the shoulder blade.

"Our enemies have fall'n, but this shall grow
A night of Summer from the heat, a breadth
Of Autumn, dropping fruits of power : and roll'd
With music in the growing breeze of Time,   40
The tops shall strike from star to star, the fangs
Shall move the stony bases of the world.

"And now, O maids, behold our sanctuary
Is violate, our laws broken : fear we not
To break them more in their behoof, whose arms   45
Champion'd our cause and won it with a day
Blanch'd in our annals, and perpetual feast,
When dames and heroines of the golden year
Shall strip a hundred hollows bare of Spring,
To rain an April of ovation round   50
Their statues, borne aloft, the three : but come,

We will be liberal, since our rights are won.
Let them not lie in the tents with coarse mankind,
Ill nurses; but descend, and proffer these
The brethren of our blood and cause, that there   55
Lie bruised and maim'd, the tender ministries
Of female hands and hospitality."

  She spoke, and with the babe yet in her arms,
Descending, burst the great bronze valves, and led
A hundred maids in train across the Park.   60
Some cowl'd, and some bare-headed, on they came,
Their feet in flowers, her loveliest: by them went
The enamor'd air sighing, and on their curls
From the high tree the blossom wavering fell,
And over them the tremulous isles of light   65
Slided, they moving under shade : but Blanche
At distance follow'd : so they came : anon
Thro' open field into the lists they wound
Timorously; and as the leader of the herd
That holds a stately fretwork to the Sun,   70
And follow'd up by a hundred airy does,
Steps with a tender foot, light as on air,
The lovely, lordly creature floated on
To where her wounded brethren lay ; there stay'd ;
Knelt on one knee, — the child on one, — and prest   75
Their hands, and call'd them dear deliverers,
And happy warriors, and immortal names,
And said " You shall not lie in the tents but here,
And nursed by those for whom you fought, and served
With female hands and hospitality."   80

  Then, whether moved by this, or was it chance,
She past my way.   Up started from my side
The old lion, glaring with his whelpless eye,
Silent; but when she saw me lying stark,

Dishelm'd and mute, and motionlessly pale,   85
Cold ev'n to her, she sigh'd; and when she saw
The haggard father's face and reverend beard
Of grisly twine, all dabbled with the blood
Of his own son, shudder'd, a twitch of pain
Tortured her mouth, and o'er her forehead past   90
A shadow, and her hue changed, and she said:
"He saved my life: my brother slew him for it."
No more: at which the king in bitter scorn
Drew from my neck the painting and the tress,
And held them up: she saw them, and a day   95
Rose from the distance on her memory,
When the good Queen, her mother, shore the tress
With kisses, ere the days of Lady Blanche:
And then once more she look'd at my pale face:
Till understanding all the foolish work   100
Of Fancy, and the bitter close of all,
Her iron will was broken in her mind;
Her noble heart was molten in her breast;
She bow'd, she set the child on the earth; she laid
A feeling finger on my brows, and presently   105
"O Sire," she said, "he lives: he is not dead:
Oh, let me have him with my brethren here
In our own palace: we will tend on him
Like one of these; if so, by any means,
To lighten this great clog of thanks, that make   110
Our progress falter to the woman's goal."

She said: but at the happy word "he lives,"
My father stoop'd, re-father'd o'er my wounds.
So those two foes above my fallen life,
With brow to brow like night and evening mixt   115
Their dark and gray, while Psyche ever stole
A little nearer, till the babe that by us,
Half-lapt in glowing gauze and golden brede,

Lay like a new-fall'n meteor on the grass,
Uncared for, spied its mother and began   120
A blind and babbling laughter, and to dance
Its body, and reach its fatling innocent arms
And lazy lingering fingers.   She the appeal
Brook'd not, but clamoring out " Mine — mine — not yours,
It is not yours, but mine : give me the child,"   125
Ceased all on tremble : piteous was the cry :
So stood the unhappy mother open-mouth'd,
And turn'd each face her way : wan was her cheek
With hollow watch, her blooming mantle torn,
Red grief and mother's hunger in her eye,   130
And down dead-heavy sank her curls, and half
The sacred mother's bosom, panting, burst
The laces toward her babe ; but she nor cared
Nor knew it, clamoring on, till Ida heard,
Look'd up, and rising slowly from me, stood   135
Erect and silent, striking with her glance
The mother, me, the child ; but he that lay
Beside us, Cyril, batter'd as he was,
Trail'd himself up on one knee ; then he drew
Her robe to meet his lips, and down she look'd   140
At the arm'd man sideways, pitying as it seem'd
Or self-involved ; but when she learnt his face,
Remembering his ill-omen'd song, arose
Once more thro' all her height, and o'er him grew
Tall as a figure lengthen'd on the sand   145
When the tide ebbs in sunshine, and he said :

" O fair and strong and terrible !   Lioness
That with your long locks play the Lion's mane !
But Love and Nature, these are two more terrible
And stronger.   See, your foot is on our necks,   150
We vanquish'd, you the Victor of your will.
What would you more ? give her the child ! remain

Orb'd in your isolation: he is dead,
Or all as dead: henceforth we let you be:
Win you the hearts of women; and beware　　　　155
Lest, where you seek the common love of these,
The common hate with the revolving wheel
Should drag you down, and some great Nemesis
Break from a darken'd future, crown'd with fire,
And tread you out for ever: but howsoe'er　　　　160
Fix'd in yourself, never in your own arms
To hold your own, deny not hers to her,
Give her the child!　Oh if, I say, you keep
One pulse that beats true woman, if you loved
The breast that fed or arm that dandled you,　　　　165
Or own one port of sense not flint to prayer,
Give her the child! or if you scorn to lay it,
Yourself, in hands so lately claspt with yours,
Or speak to her, your dearest, her one fault
The tenderness, not yours, that could not kill,　　　　170
Give *me* it: *I* will give it her."
　　　　　　　　　　　He said:
At first her eye with slow dilation roll'd
Dry flame, she listening; after sank and sank
And, into mournful twilight mellowing, dwelt
Full on the child; she took it: "Pretty bud!　　　　175
Lily of the vale! half open'd bell of the woods!
Sole comfort of my dark hour, when a world
Of traitorous friend and broken system made
No purple in the distance, mystery,
Pledge of a love not to be mine, farewell;　　　　180
These men are hard upon us as of old;
We two must part: and yet how fain was I
To dream thy cause embraced in mine, to think
I might be something to thee, when I felt
Thy helpless warmth about my barren breast　　　　185
In the dead prime: but may thy mother prove

As true to thee as false, false, false to me!
And, if thou needs must bear the yoke, I wish it
Gentle as freedom" — here she kiss'd it: then —
" All good go with thee! take it, Sir," and so   190
Laid the soft babe in his hard-mailed hands,
Who turn'd half-round to Psyche as she sprang
To meet it, with an eye that swum in thanks;
Then felt it sound and whole from head to foot,
And hugg'd and never hugg'd it close enough,   195
And in her hunger mouth'd and mumbled it,
And hid her bosom with it; after that
Put on more calm and added suppliantly:

  " We two were friends: I go to mine own land
For ever: find some other: as for me   200
I scarce am fit for your great plans: yet speak to me,
Say one soft word and let me part forgiven."

  But Ida spoke not, rapt upon the child.
Then Arac. " Ida — 's death! you blame the man;
You wrong yourselves — the woman is so hard   205
Upon the woman.   Come, a grace to me!
I am your warrior: I and mine have fought
Your battle: kiss her; take her hand, she weeps:
'S death!   I would sooner fight thrice o'er than see it."

  But Ida spoke not, gazing on the ground,   210
And reddening in the furrows of his chin,
And moved beyond his custom, Gama said:

  " I've heard that there is iron in the blood,
And I believe it.   Not one word? not one?
Whence drew you this steel temper? not from me,   215
Not from your mother, now a saint with saints.
She said you had a heart — I heard her say it —

'Our Ida has a heart' — just ere she died —
'But see that some one with authority
Be near her still' and I — I sought for one —   220
All people said she had authority —
The Lady Blanche: much profit! Not one word;
No! tho' your father sues: see how you stand
Stiff as Lot's wife, and all the good knights maim'd,
I trust that there is no one hurt to death,   225
For your wild whim: and was it then for this,
Was it for this we gave our palace up,
Where we withdrew from summer heats and state,
And had our wine and chess beneath the planes,
And many a pleasant hour with her that's gone,   230
Ere you were born to vex us? Is it kind?
Speak to her I say: is this not she of whom,
When first she came, all flush'd you said to me
Now had you got a friend of your own age,
Now could you share your thought; now should men see
Two women faster welded in one love   236
Than pairs of wedlock; she you walk'd with, she
You talk'd with, whole nights long, up in the tower,
Of sine and arc, spheroïd and azimuth,
And right ascension, Heaven knows what; and now   240
A word, but one, one little kindly word,
Not one to spare her: out upon you, flint!
You love nor her, nor me, nor any; nay,
You shame your mother's judgment too. Not one?
You will not? well — no heart have you, or such   245
As fancies like the vermin in a nut
Have fretted all to dust and bitterness."
So said the small king moved beyond his wont.

But Ida stood nor spoke, drain'd of her force
By many a varying influence and so long.   250
Down thro' her limbs a drooping languor wept:

Her head a little bent; and on her mouth
A doubtful smile dwelt like a clouded moon
In a still water: then brake out my sire. "O you,   255
Woman, whom we thought woman even now,
And were half fool'd to let you tend our son,
Because he might have wish'd it — but we see
The accomplice of your madness unforgiven,
And think that you might mix his draught with death   260
When your skies change again: the rougher hand
Is safer: on to the tents: take up the Prince."

He rose, and while each ear was prick'd to attend
A tempest, thro' the cloud that dimm'd her broke
A genial warmth and light once more, and shone   265
Thro' glittering drops on her sad friend.
                                        "Come hither,
O Psyche!" she cried out; "embrace me, come,
Quick while I melt; make reconcilement sure
With one that cannot keep her mind an hour:
Come to the hollow heart they slander so!   270
Kiss and be friends, like children being chid!
I seem no more: *I* want forgiveness too:
I should have had to do with none but maids,
That have no links with men. Ah false but dear,
Dear traitor, too much loved, why? — why? — Yet see,   275
Before these kings we embrace you yet once more
With all forgiveness, all oblivion,
And trust, not love, you less.
                            And now, O Sire,
Grant me your son, to nurse, to wait upon him,
Like mine own brother. For my debt to him,   280
This nightmare weight of gratitude, I know it;
Taunt me no more: yourself and yours shall have
Free adit; we will scatter all our maids

Till happier times each to her proper hearth:
What use to keep them here — now ? Grant my prayer. 285
Help, father, brother, help; speak to the king :
Thaw this male nature to some touch of that
Which kills me with myself, and drags me down
From my fixt height to mob me up with all
The soft and milky rabble of womankind,   290
Poor weakling ev'n as they are."

                               Passionate tears
Follow'd: the king replied not: Cyril said:
" Your brother, Lady, — Florian, — ask for him
Of your great head — for he is wounded too —
That you may tend upon him with the prince."   295
" Ay so," said Ida with a bitter smile,
" Our laws are broken: let him enter too."
Then Violet, she that sang the mournful song,
And had a cousin tumbled on the plain,
Petition'd too for him. " Ay so," she said,   300
" I stagger in the stream: I cannot keep
My heart an eddy from the brawling hour:
We break our laws with ease, but let it be."
"Ay so?" said Blanche: "Amazed am I to hear
Your Highness: but your Highness breaks with ease   305
The law your Highness did not make: 'twas I.
I had been wedded wife, I knew mankind,
And block'd them out; but these men came to woo
Your Highness — verily I think to win."

  So she, and turn'd askance a wintry eye :   310
But Ida with a voice, that like a bell
Toll'd by an earthquake in a trembling tower,
Rang ruin, answer'd full of grief and scorn.

  " Fling our doors wide ! all, all, not one, but all,
Not only he, but by my mother's soul,   315

Whatever man lies wounded, friend or foe,
Shall enter, if he will.   Let our girls flit,
Till the storm die! but had you stood by us,
The roar that breaks the Pharos from his base
Had left us rock.   She fain would sting us too,   320
But shall not.   Pass, and mingle with your likes.
We brook no further insult but are gone."

    She turn'd; the very nape of her white neck
Was rosed with indignation: but the Prince
Her brother came; the king her father charm'd   325
Her wounded soul with words: nor did mine own
Refuse her proffer, lastly gave his hand.

    Then us they lifted up, dead weights, and bare
Straight to the doors: to them the doors gave way
Groaning, and in the Vestal entry shriek'd   330
The virgin marble under iron heels:
And on they moved and gain'd the hall, and there
Rested: but great the crush was, and each base,
To left and right, of those tall columns drown'd
In silken fluctuation and the swarm   335
Of female whisperers: at the further end
Was Ida by the throne, the two great cats
Close by her, like supporters on a shield,
Bow-back'd with fear: but in the center stood
The common men with rolling eyes; amazed   340
They glared upon the women, and aghast
The women stared at these, all silent, save
When armor clash'd or jingled, while the day,
Descending, struck athwart the hall, and shot
A flying splendor out of brass and steel,   345
That o'er the statues leapt from head to head,
Now fired an angry Pallas on the helm,
Now set a wrathful Dian's moon on flame,

And now and then an echo started up,
And shuddering fled from room to room, and died   350
Of fright in far apartments.
       Then the voice
Of Ida sounded, issuing ordinance:
And me they bore up the broad stairs, and thro'
The long-laid galleries past a hundred doors
To one deep chamber shut from sound, and due   355
To languid limbs and sickness; left me in it;
And others otherwhere they laid; and all
That afternoon a sound arose of hoof
And chariot, many a maiden passing home
Till happier times; but some were left of those   360
Held sagest, and the great lords out and in,
From those two hosts that lay beside the walls,
Walk'd at their will, and everything was changed.

  Ask me no more: the moon may draw the sea;
   The cloud may stoop from heaven and take the shape,
    With fold to fold, of mountain or of cape;
  But O too fond! when have I answered thee?
     Ask me no more.

  Ask me no more: what answer should I give?
   I love not hollow cheek or faded eye:
   Yet, O my friend, I will not have thee die!
  Ask me no more, lest I should bid thee live;
     Ask me no more.

  Ask me no more: thy fate and mine are seal'd:
   I strove against the stream and all in vain:
   Let the great river take me to the main:
  No more, dear love, for at a touch I yield;
     Ask me no more.

Canto VII.

So was their sanctuary violated,
So their fair college turn'd to hospital ;
At first with all confusion : by and by
Sweet order lived again with other laws :
A kindlier influence reign'd ; and everywhere   5
Low voices with the ministering hand
Hung round the sick : the maidens came, they talk'd,
They sang, they read : till she not fair began
To gather light, and she that was became
Her former beauty treble ; and to and fro   10
With books, with flowers, with Angel offices,
Like creatures native unto gracious act,
And in their own clear element, they moved.

But sadness on the soul of Ida fell,
And hatred of her weakness, blent with shame.   15
Old studies fail'd ; seldom she spoke : but oft
Clomb to the roofs, and gazed alone for hours
On that disastrous leaguer, swarms of men
Darkening her female field : void was her use,
And she as one that climbs a peak to gaze   20
O'er land and main, and sees a great black cloud
Drag inward from the deeps, a wall of night,
Blot out the slope of sea from verge to shore,
And suck the blinding splendor from the sand,
And quenching lake by lake and tarn by tarn   25
Expunge the world : so fared she gazing there ;
So blacken'd all her world in secret, blank
And waste it seem'd and vain ; till down she came,
And found fair peace once more among the sick.

And twilight dawn'd ; and morn by morn the lark   30
Shot up and shrill'd in flickering gyres, but I

Lay silent in the muffled cage of life :
And twilight gloom'd ; and broader-grown the bowers
Drew the great night into themselves, and Heaven,
Star after star, arose and fell ; but I,   35
Deeper than those weird doubts could reach me, lay
Quite sunder'd from the moving Universe,
Nor knew what eye was on me, nor the hand
That nursed me, more than infants in their sleep.

    But Psyche tended Florian : with her oft,   40
Melissa came ; for Blanche had gone, but left
Her child among us, willing she should keep
Court-favor : here and there the small bright head,
A light of healing, glanced about the couch,
Or thro' the parted silks the tender face   45
Peep'd, shining in upon the wounded man
With blush and smile, a medicine in themselves
To wile the length from languorous hours, and draw
The sting from pain ; nor seem'd it strange that soon
He rose up whole, and those fair charities   50
Join'd at her side ; nor stranger seem'd that hearts
So gentle, so employ'd, should close in love,
Than when two dewdrops on the petal shake
To the same sweet air, and tremble deeper down,
And slip at once all-fragrant into one.   55

    Less prosperously the second suit obtain'd
At first with Psyche.   Not tho' Blanche had sworn
That after that dark night among the fields
She needs must wed him for her own good name ;
Not tho' he built upon the babe restored ;   60
Nor tho' she liked him, yielded she, but fear'd
To incense the Head once more ; till on a day
When Cyril pleaded, Ida came behind
Seen but of Psyche : on her foot she hung

A moment, and she heard, at which her face 65
A little flush'd, and she passed on; but each
Assumed from thence a half-consent involved
In stillness, plighted troth, and were at peace.

Nor only these: Love in the sacred halls *men bane wrote*
Held carnival at will, and flying struck 70
With showers of random sweet on maid and man.
Nor did her father cease to press my claim,
Nor did mine own now reconciled; nor yet
Did those twin brothers, risen again and whole;
Nor Arac, satiate with his victory. 75

But I lay still, and with me oft she sat:
Then came a change; for sometimes I would catch
Her hand in wild delirium, gripe it hard,
And fling it like a viper off, and shriek
"You are not Ida"; clasp it once again, 80
And call her Ida, tho' I knew her not;
And call her sweet, as if in irony;
And call her hard and cold, which seem'd a truth:
And still she fear'd that I should lose my mind,
And often she believed that I should die: 85
Till out of long frustration of her care,
And pensive tendance in the all-weary noons,
And watches in the dead, the dark, when clocks
Throbb'd thunder thro' the palace floors, or call'd
On flying Time from all their silver tongues— 90
And out of memories of her kindlier days,
And sidelong glances at my father's grief,
And at the happy lovers heart in heart—
And out of hauntings of my spoken love,
And lonely listenings to my mutter'd dream, 95
And often feeling of the helpless hands,
And wordless broodings on the wasted cheek—

From all a closer interest flourish'd up,
Tenderness touch by touch, and last, to these,
Love, like an Alpine harebell hung with tears   100
By some cold morning glacier; frail at first
And feeble, all unconscious of itself,
But such as gather'd color day by day.

   Last I woke sane, but well-nigh close to death
For weakness: it was evening: silent light   105
Slept on the painted walls, wherein were wrought
Two grand designs; for on one side arose
The women up in wild revolt, and storm'd
At the Oppian law.   Titanic shapes, they cramm'd
The forum, and half-crush'd among the rest   110
A dwarf-like Cato cower'd.   On the other side
Hortensia spoke against the tax; behind,
A train of dames: by ax and eagle sat,
With all their foreheads drawn in Roman scowls,
And half the wolf's milk curdled in their veins,   115
The fierce triumvirs; and before them paused
Hortensia pleading: angry was her face.

   I saw the forms: I knew not where I was:
They did but look like hollow shows; nor more
Sweet Ida: palm to palm she sat: the dew   120
Dwelt in her eyes, and softer all her shape
And rounder seem'd: I moved: I sigh'd: a touch
Came round my wrist, and tears upon my hand:
Then all for languor and self-pity ran
Mine down my face, and with what life I had,   125
And like a flower that cannot all unfold,
So drench'd it is with tempest, to the sun,
Yet, as it may, turns toward him, I on her
Fixt my faint eyes, and utter'd whisperingly:

"If you be, what I think you, some sweet dream,   130
I would but ask you to fulfill yourself:
But if you be that Ida whom I knew,
I ask you nothing: only, if a dream,
Sweet dream, be perfect.   I shall die to-night.
Stoop down, and seem to kiss me ere I die."   135

I could no more, but lay like one in trance,
That hears his burial talk'd of by his friends,
And cannot speak, nor move, nor make one sign,
But lies and dreads his doom.   She turn'd; she paused;
She stoop'd; and out of languor leapt a cry;   140
Leapt fiery Passion from the brinks of death;
And I believed that in the living world
My spirit closed with Ida's at the lips;
Till back I fell, and from mine arms she rose
Glowing all over noble shame; and all   145
Her falser self slipt from her like a robe,
And left her woman, lovelier in her mood
Than in her mold that other, when she came
From barren deeps to conquer all with love;
And down the streaming crystal dropt; and she   150
Far-fleeted by the purple island-sides,
Naked, a double light in air and wave,
To meet her Graces, where they deck'd her out
For worship without end; nor end of mine,
Stateliest, for thee! but mute she glided forth,   155
Nor glanced behind her, and I sank and slept,
Fill'd thro' and thro' with Love, a happy sleep.

Deep in the night I woke: she, near me, held
A volume of the Poets of her land:
There to herself, all in low tones, she read.   160

"Now sleeps the crimson petal, now the white;
Nor waves the cypress in the palace walk;

Nor winks the gold fin in the porphyry font:
The fire-fly wakens: waken thou with me.

Now droops the milk-white peacock like a ghost,   165
And like a ghost she glimmers on to me.

Now lies the Earth all Danaë to the stars,
And all thy heart lies open unto me.

Now slides the silent meteor on, and leaves
A shining furrow, as thy thoughts in me.   170

Now folds the lily all her sweetness up,
And slips into the bosom of the lake:
So fold thyself, my dearest, thou, and slip
Into my bosom and be lost in me."

I heard her turn the page; she found a small   175
Sweet idyl, and once more, as low, she read:

"Come down, O maid, from yonder mountain height:
What pleasure lives in height (the shepherd sang)
In height and cold, the splendor of the hills ?
But cease to move so near the Heavens, and cease   180
To glide a sunbeam by the blasted Pine,
To sit a star upon the sparkling spire ;
And come, for Love is of the valley, come,
For Love is of the valley, come thou down
And find him ; by the happy threshold, he,   185
Or hand in hand with Plenty in the maize,
Or red with spirted purple of the vats,
Or foxlike in the vine ; nor cares to walk
With Death and Morning on the silver horns,
Nor wilt thou snare him in the white ravine,   190
Nor find him dropt upon the firths of ice,
That huddling slant in furrow-cloven falls
To roll the torrent out of dusky doors:
But follow ; let the torrent dance thee down
To find him in the valley ; let the wild   195
Lean-headed Eagles yelp alone, and leave
The monstrous ledges there to slope, and spill
Their thousand wreaths of dangling water-smoke,

That like a broken purpose waste in air:
So waste not thou; but come; for all the vales   200
Await thee; azure pillars of the hearth
Arise to thee; the children call, and I
Thy shepherd pipe, and sweet is every sound,
Sweeter thy voice, but every sound is sweet;
Myriads of rivulets hurrying thro' the lawn,   205
The moan of doves in immemorial elms,
And murmuring of innumerable bees."

So she low-toned; while with shut eyes I lay
Listening; then look'd. Pale was the perfect face;
The bosom with long sighs labor'd; and meek   210
Seem'd the full lips, and mild the luminous eyes,
And the voice trembled and the hand. She said
Brokenly, that she knew it, she had fail'd
In sweet humility; had fail'd in all;
That all her labor was but as a block   215
Left in the quarry; but she still were loth,
She still were loth to yield herself to one
That wholly scorn'd to help their equal rights
Against the sons of men, and barbarous laws.
She pray'd me not to judge their cause from her   220
That wrong'd it, sought far less for truth than power
In knowledge: something wild within her breast,
A greater than all knowledge, beat her down.
And she had nursed me there from week to week:
Much had she learnt in little time. In part   225
It was ill counsel had misled the girl
To vex true hearts: yet was she but a girl —
"Ah fool, and made myself a Queen of farce!
When comes another such? never, I think,
Till the Sun drop, dead, from the signs."
                                        Her voice   230
Choked, and her forehead sank upon her hands,
And her great heart thro' all the faultful Past

Went sorrowing in a pause I dared not break;
Till notice of a change in the dark world
Was lispt about the acacias, and a bird,   235
That early woke to feed her little ones,
Sent from a dewy breast a cry for light:
She moved, and at her feet the volume fell.

  " Blame not thyself too much," I said, " nor blame
Too much the sons of men and barbarous laws;   240
These were the rough ways of the world till now.
Henceforth thou hast a helper, me, that know
The woman's cause is man's: they rise or sink
Together, dwarf'd or godlike, bond or free:
For she that out of Lethe scales with man   245
The shining steps of Nature, shares with man
His nights, his days, moves with him to one goal,
Stays all the fair young planet in her hands —
If she be small, slight-natured, miserable,
How shall men grow? but work no more alone!   250
Our place is much: as far as in us lies
We two will serve them both in aiding her —
Will clear away the parasitic forms
That seem to keep her up but drag her down —
Will leave her space to burgeon out of all   255
Within her — let her make herself her own
To give or keep, to live and learn and be
All that not harms distinctive womanhood.
For woman is not undevelopt man,
But diverse: could we make her as the man,   260
Sweet Love were slain: his dearest bond is this,
Not like to like, but like in difference.
Yet in the long years liker must they grow
The man be more of woman, she of man;
He gain in sweetness and in moral height,   265
Nor lose the wrestling thews that throw the world;

She mental breadth, nor fail in childward care,
Nor lose the childlike in the larger mind;
Till at the last she set herself to man,
Like perfect music unto noble words;   270
And so these twain, upon the skirts of Time,
Sit side by side, full-summ'd in all their powers,
Dispensing harvest, sowing the To-be,
Self-reverent each and reverencing each,
Distinct in individualities,   275
But like each other ev'n as those who love.
Then comes the statelier Eden back to men:
Then reigns the world's great bridals, chaste and calm:
Then springs the crowning race of humankind.
May these things be!"

                       Sighing she spoke, "I fear   280
They will not."

                  "Dear, but let us type them now
In our own lives, and this proud watchword rest
Of equal; seeing either sex alone
Is half itself, and in true marriage lies
Nor equal, nor unequal: each fulfills   285
Defect in each, and always thought in thought,
Purpose in purpose, will in will, they grow,
The single pure and perfect animal,
The two-cell'd heart beating, with one full stroke,
Life."

              And again sighing she spoke: "A dream   290
That once was mine! what woman taught you this?"

"Alone," I said, "from earlier than I know,
Immersed in rich foreshadowings of the world,
I loved the woman: he, that doth not, lives
A drowning life, besotted in sweet self,   295
Or pines in sad experience worse than death,
Or keeps his wing'd affections clipt with crime:

Yet was there one thro' whom I loved her, one
Not learned, save in gracious household ways,
Not perfect, nay, but full of tender wants,   300
No Angel, but a dearer being, all dipt
In Angel instincts, breathing Paradise,
Interpreter between the Gods and men,
Who look'd all native to her place, and yet
On tiptoe seem'd to touch upon a sphere   305
Too gross to tread, and all male minds perforce
Sway'd to her from their orbits as they moved,
And girdled her with music.   Happy he
With such a mother! faith in womankind
Beats with his blood, and trust in all things high   310
Comes easy to him, and tho' he trip and fall
He shall not blind his soul with clay."

                                              " But I,"

Said Ida, tremulously, " so all unlike —
It seems you love to cheat yourself with words:
This mother is your model.   I have heard   315
Of your strange doubts: they well might be: I seem
A mockery to my own self.   Never, Prince;
You cannot love me."

                              "Nay but thee," I said,
" From yearlong poring on thy pictured eyes,
Ere seen I loved, and loved thee seen, and saw   320
Thee woman thro' the crust of iron moods
That mask'd thee from men's reverence up, and forced
Sweet love on pranks of saucy boyhood: now,
Giv'n back to life, to life indeed, thro' thee,
Indeed I love : the new day comes, the light   325
Dearer for night, as dearer thou for faults
Lived over: lift thine eyes; my doubts are dead,
My haunting sense of hollow shows: the change,
This truthful change in thee has kill'd it.   Dear,
Look up, and let thy nature strike on mine,   330

Like yonder morning on the blind half-world;
Approach and fear not; breathe upon my brows;
In that fine air I tremble, all the past
Melts mist-like into this bright hour, and this
Is morn to more, and all the rich to-come   335
Reels, as the golden Autumn woodland reels
Athwart the smoke of burning weeds.   Forgive me,
I waste my heart in signs: let be.   My bride,
My wife, my life.   Oh, we will walk this world,
Yoked in all exercise of noble end,   340
And so thro' those dark gates across the wild
That no man knows.   Indeed I love thee: come,
Yield thyself up: my hopes and thine are one:
Accomplish thou my manhood and thyself;
Lay thy sweet hands in mine and trust to me."   345

CONCLUSION.

So closed our tale, of which I give you all
The random scheme as wildly as it rose:
The words are mostly mine; for when we ceased
There came a minute's pause, and Walter said,
"I wish she had not yielded!" then to me,   5
"What, if you drest it up poetically!"
So pray'd the men, the women: I gave assent:
Yet how to bind the scatter'd scheme of seven
Together in one sheaf?   What style could suit?
The men required that I should give throughout   10
The sort of mock-heroic gigantesque,
With which we banter'd little Lilia first:
The women — and perhaps they felt their power,
For something in the ballads which they sang,
Or in their silent influence as they sat,   15
Had ever seem'd to wrestle with burlesque,
And drove us, last, to quite a solemn close —

They hated banter, wish'd for something real,
A gallant fight, a noble princess — why
Not make her true-heroic — true-sublime ?   20
Or all, they said, as earnest as the close ?
Which yet with such a framework scarce could be.
Then rose a little feud betwixt the two,
Betwixt the mockers and the realists:
And I, betwixt them both, to please them both,   25
And yet to give the story as it rose,
I moved as in a strange diagonal,
And maybe neither pleased myself nor them.

But Lilia pleased me, for she took no part
In our dispute: the sequel of the tale   30
Had touch'd her; and she sat, she pluck'd the grass,
She flung it from her, thinking: last, she fixt
A showery glance upon her aunt, and said,
"You — tell us what we are," who might have told,
For she was cramm'd with theories out of books,   35
But that there rose a shout: the gates were closed
At sunset, and the crowd were swarming now,
To take their leave, about the garden rails.

So I and some went out to these: we climb'd
The slope to Vivian-place, and turning saw   40
The happy valleys, half in light, and half
Far-shadowing from the west, a land of peace;
Gray halls alone among their massive groves;
Trim hamlets; here and there a rustic tower
Half-lost in belts of hop and breadths of wheat;   45
The shimmering glimpses of a stream; the seas;
A red sail, or a white; and far beyond,
Imagined more than seen, the skirts of France.

"Look there, a garden!" said my college friend,
The Tory member's elder son, "and there!   50

God bless the narrow sea which keeps her off,
And keeps our Britain, whole within herself,
A nation yet, the rulers and the ruled —
Some sense of duty, something of a faith,
Some reverence for the laws ourselves have made,　　55
Some patient force to change them when we will,
Some civic manhood firm against the crowd —
But yonder, whiff! there comes a sudden heat,
The gravest citizen seems to lose his head,
The king is scared, the soldier will not fight,　　60
The little boys begin to shoot and stab,
A kingdom topples over with a shriek
Like an old woman, and down rolls the world
In mock heroics stranger than our own;
Revolts, republics, revolutions, most　　65
No graver than a schoolboy's barring out;
Too comic for the solemn things they are,
Too solemn for the comic touches in them,
Like our wild Princess with as wise a dream
As some of theirs — God bless the narrow seas!　　70
I wish they were a whole Atlantic broad."

　"Have patience," I replied, " ourselves are full
Of social wrong; and maybe wildest dreams
Are but the needful preludes of the truth:
For me, the genial day, the happy crowd,　　75
The sport half-science, fill me with a faith.
This fine old world of ours is but a child
Yet in the go-cart.　Patience!　Give it time
To learn its limbs: there is a hand that guides."

　In such discourse we gain'd the garden rails,　　80
And there we saw Sir Walter where he stood,
Before a tower of crimson holly-hoaks,
Among six boys, head under head, and look'd
No little lily-handed Baronet he,

A great broad-shoulder'd genial Englishman,   85
A lord of fat prize-oxen and of sheep,
A raiser of huge melons and of pine,
A patron of some thirty charities,
A pamphleteer on guano and on grain,
A quarter-sessions chairman, abler none;   90
Fair-hair'd and redder than a windy morn;
Now shaking hands with him, now him, of those
That stood the nearest — now address'd to speech —
Who spoke few words and pithy, such as closed
Welcome, farewell, and welcome for the year   95
To follow: a shout rose again, and made
The long line of the approaching rookery swerve
From the elms, and shook the branches of the deer
From slope to slope thro' distant ferns, and rang
Beyond the bourn of sunset; oh, a shout   100
More joyful than the city roar that hails
Premier or king! Why should not these great Sirs
Give up their parks some dozen times a year
To let the people breathe? So thrice they cried,
I likewise, and in groups they stream'd away.   105

But we went back to the Abbey, and sat on,
So much the gathering darkness charm'd: we sat
But spoke not, rapt in nameless reverie,
Perchance upon the future man: the walls
Blacken'd about us, bats wheel'd, and owls whoop'd,   110
And gradually the powers of the night,
That range above the region of the wind,
Deepening the courts of twilight broke them up
Thro' all the silent spaces of the worlds,
Beyond all thought into the Heaven of Heavens.   115

Last little Lilia, rising quietly,
Disrobed the glimmering statue of Sir Ralph
From those rich silks, and home well-pleased we went.

NOTES.

———•◦•———

Many of the following notes have not hitherto appeared in any edition of "The Princess," so far as the editor is aware ; others have been used in numerous editions until they have become common property. The editor has availed himself freely of all material within his reach, and acknowledges his indebtedness to the commentators who have preceded him.

Prologue.

Line 1. The scene is here laid in the grounds of an English country-seat, said to be that of Sir John Simeon, at Swainston, which the owner had opened for the day to his tenantry and to the Mechanics' Institute of the neighboring borough, or town, for a field meeting. The poet represents himself as visiting at the house with a party of college friends, who gather in the Abbey ruin, and there tell the story of "The Princess," each taking up a part in succession, in round robin fashion. The Prologue is an introduction, of which the purpose is to open the subject, to provide the occasion and the scenery of the tale, and to give the atmosphere which shall develop it. The description of the landscape, with its medley of mimic experiments in popular science, its reflection of new conditions of common education, and its general air of novelty and contemporary change, gives the background of the smaller party in the Abbey ruin, but also fitly prepares the mind for the subjects of thought with which the poem deals. The description of the house and the Abbey ruin, on the other hand, is more narrowly intended to lead up to the contrasts, the jumble of elements, and general miscellaneousness of the narrative itself. "I have every reason to believe that the mansion referred to in Tennyson's 'Princess' belongs to the Lushington family, and is near Maidstone. I was present at a fête of the Maidstone Mechanics' Institute, and took part in several of the experiments referred to, and the description exactly agrees with what occurred " (adapted).

Line 2. "Lawns." The modern usage of this word generally con-

127

veys the idea of closely-mown grass in a well-kept garden; in this passage it has the older meaning of an extent of natural pasture land or untilled glade, such as contributes so much to the charm of an English country gentleman's park.

Line 5. The local People's "Institute," with its half-social, half-educational aims, was then, and is now, a power in England.

Line 11. "Greek." A house built after a Greek model has generally a main front, adorned with pillars or pilasters and a pediment, and flanked with wings. This style of architecture came into fashion in England about the middle of the eighteenth century.

Line 14. "The Abbey ruin." After the suppression of the English monasteries by Henry VIII., the old buildings fell into decay, and subsequent owners of the estates have not unfrequently even made use of the old materials in the construction of new houses.

Line 15. "Ammonites." Large fossils, with the appearance of coiled snakes. — "First bones of Time." The fossil bones of the earliest animals preserved to us.

Line 16. "Every clime and age," *i.e.* their products.

Line 20. "Laborious orient ivory." Referring to those marvels of Chinese ivory cutting, consisting of carved balls within balls. The line is a striking example of the correspondence of sound and sense, the words seeming to roll round like the "sphere in sphere."

Line 21. "Crease." A heavy dagger, called "cursed" because of the terrible gashed wound it makes, owing to its form; it has a waved blade set in the handle obliquely.

Line 26. "Ascalon." A city on the Mediterranean, southwest of Jerusalem. It was taken by the Crusaders in 1099, and a second time in 1192, when Richard Cœur de Lion gained a great victory over the Saracens led by Saladin.

Line 31. "Laid about them at their wills." Smote right and left with vigor, lived strong warrior lives. Fighting merely for fighting's sake, in the absence of any other inducement, was not an uncommon form of recreation among the gentlemen of Europe in mediæval times.

Line 35. "Miracle." A stronger word for *marvel*. The exact meaning is a woman so surpassing in character as to seem above the reach of nature to produce.

Line 64. "Wisp." A meteoric light which dances above the ground, chiefly in marshy places. In legend it is a lamp carried by Will-o'-the-wisp, or Jack-o'-lantern, to lead travelers into dangerous places.

Lines 68–70. "A group of girls," etc. A circle of girls is formed, at one point of which is placed an electric battery, the girl on each side grasping a handle. The current is turned on, and the shock, communicated throughout, causes each to drop the hands she is holding.

Line 86. "Soldier-laddie" —

> "My soger laddie is over the sea,
> And he will bring gold and siller to me."

A favorite Scotch song, printed in Cunningham's "Songs of Scotland."

Line 89. "Smacking of the time." Typical of the age, as indicating the spread of scientific interests among the people.

Line 92. "Gothic" architecture is characterized by lightness and delicacy. It prevailed in England in the thirteenth and fourteenth centuries.

Line 108. "Took this fair day." An expression derived from the custom of preachers, who take a passage from the Bible and enlarge upon it, drawing out its full meaning and moral.

Line 109. "The crowd" is here used for "the lower classes."

Lines 111–113. "He had climb'd." The Oxford or Cambridge man does not care to be caught out of bounds by the proctor. Mr. Richard Harding Davis tells of one who had surprised the dignitaries by his skill in surmounting the wall, and escaped being suspended on condition that he would divulge the means by which he did it. This he did by informing them that they would find his answer in the eighteenth Psalm, twenty-ninth verse : "By [the help of] my God have I leaped over a wall." Mr. Davis says that the means of escape is "sometimes a coal-hole, sometimes a tree whose branches stretch over the spiked wall, and sometimes a sloping roof."

Line 113. "Breath'd the proctor's dogs." Made the attendants of the proctor run until they were out of breath. A proctor is a university or college officer whose duty it is to keep good order.

Line 114. "Tutor." An officer in charge of both education and discipline, and an adviser of students under him.

Line 116. "Master." Head of a college.

Line 128. "Convention." Conventionality, custom.

Lines 134–135. "I would build . . . like a man's." This sentence strikes the keynote of the poem. It contains the pith of the whole matter.

Line 144. "Emperor-moths." A handsome species common in England.

Line 161. "Lost their weeks." An English undergraduate must

be in actual residence at his college a certain number of terms, as a
condition of receiving a degree.   By absence, beyond a certain limit,
"they lose their weeks"; that is, they cannot count the term in which
such absences occur as a part of their residence.

Line 163.   "Caught the blossom of the flying terms."   Enjoyed
to the utmost the fresh pleasures of the days as they sped by.

Line 176.   "Stay'd . . . up."   Remained at the college instead of
going home for the vacation.   "To read" is the term generally used
at the English universities for *to study*.

Line 178.   Mathematics.

Lines 183–184.   "Pledge you all in wassail."   Drink to your healths.

Lines 187–188.   The references are to popular games involving the
exercise of ingenuity and skill in analysis.

Line 192.   "Magic music" and "forfeits" are games of a more
boisterous character.

Line 229.   "Burnt," for witchcraft.

Canto I.   Line 1.   The first speaker here begins the story.

Line 7.   "Cast no shadow."   The myth of the man who cast no
shadow is not uncommon in modern literature.   In the present
instance the sorcerer had no shadow because he had sold his soul to
Satan, on the theory explained in the following passage: "To under-
stand the popular conceptions of the human soul or spirit, it is in-
structive to notice the words which have been found suitable to
express it.   The ghost or phantasm seen by the dreamer or the vision-
ary is like a shadow, and thus the familiar term of the *shade* comes in
to express the soul."

Line 19.   Claudius "Galen," of Pergamus, the most remarkable
medical authority of ancient times, has left his name to posterity as a
synonym for an eminent physician.

Line 23.   "Half-canonized."   Regarded as almost a saint.

Line 27.   "Pedant."   The older meaning of this word is *schoolmaster*.

Line 33.   "Proxy-wedded with a bootless calf."   Wedded to a
substitute who represented the Prince.   Such marriages sometimes
took place in the Middle Ages, and so late as at the end of the fifteenth
century.   "With a bootless calf" refers to a part of such ceremony
which was occasionally undertaken, the substitute or proxy of the
bridegroom appearing in the presence of the bride with "his leg stript
naked to the knee."

Line 56.   "Twinn'd."   Forming a perfect pair, acting together in
complete unison.

Lines 64–65. " Chew'd the thrice-turn'd cud of wrath." Let his heart feed again upon its indignation, turning the insult over in his mind. The expression is one that we have derived from the Latin, and is a metaphor from the habit that cows and other " ruminants " have of re-chewing food already once swallowed.

Line 65. " Cook'd his spleen." A literal translation of a classical phrase meaning *nursed his wrath*, suppressing it until some action should be decided upon.

Line 85. " I grate on rusty hinges here." My idle life here is irksome to me. The metaphor is from a gate that through long disuse is not easily opened or shut.

Line 86. " We ourself." The royal style of speech used throughout the poem by the Kings and the Princess.

Line 100. " Ere the silver sickle." Before the new moon had grown full.

Line 106. " Bastion'd." A bastion is a particular kind of fortification.

Line 109. " Tilth." Tilled ground. — " Grange." An outlying farm estate, with special reference to its cluster of buildings.

Line 110. " Blowing bosks." Blossoming wild shrubs in thickets.

Line 111. " Mother-city." The metropolis, or capital city.

Line 116. " Without a star." With no decoration of the orders of nobility.

Line 120. " Signet gem." A seal ring, the token of his authority.

Line 134. " Knowledge, so my daughter held." Some have thought this, and the general idea of the poem, borrowed from Johnson's " Rasselas " : " The princess thought that of all sublunary things knowledge was the best : she desired, first, to learn all sciences, and then proposed to found a college of learned women, in which she would preside, that, by conversing with the old, and educating the young, she might divide her time between the acquisition and communication of wisdom, and raise up for the next age models of prudence and patterns of piety."

Line 135. " Was all in all." " This fallacy, upon which is based the fore-doomed scheme of the Princess for the betterment of woman's position, is one upon which Tennyson has expressed himself, with great vehemence and earnestness, in several passages throughout his works. Knowledge, he teaches, is good, but it is not the best. The best is Wisdom. Mere Knowledge is brutal and overweening ; Wisdom is reverent and serene. This sane and wholesome doctrine of the insufficiency and dangerousness of Knowledge without the restraint and guidance of a higher power, finds its most splendid and vigorous expression in ' In Memoriam,' CXIV., which should be carefully studied. More specially is the fallacy disastrous when taken in connection with the Lady Ida's mistaken analogy on the subject of education for the two sexes. The province of woman in the economy of Nature is not intellectual eminence, but the more graceful and tender offices of life, and this, the established verdict of centuries, is the central idea and doctrine of the Poem " (Wallace).

Line 151. "They see no men." The Princess makes three mistakes, each fatal to the success of her scheme. They are : (1) " Knowledge, so my daughter held, was all in all " (line 134) ; (2) "They must lose the child, assume the woman" (line 136) ; (3) " They see no men " (line 151). Stopford Brooke has made some very suggestive comments on these three mistakes of the Princess. He says : "All the work of the world ought to be done by both of the sexes in harmonious and equal coöperation, each sex taking what fits best its hand. Without this union the world's work is only half done. And with regard to the woman's cause itself, it can make no progress as long as the law that in all work both sexes should labor together is disobeyed."

Line 163. " Frets." Hindrances.

Line 170. " Liberties." An English legal term for adjacent privileged territory ; here used of the outskirts of the estate within which the exclusive rights granted to the Princess were exercised.

Line 171. " Hostel." Hostelry, or tavern.

Line 174. " Sibilation." Not so loud as to be a whistle.

Line 181. " Summer of the vine." The genial heat of the wine.

Line 187. " To post." To arrange a service of horses for those traveling by stages.

Line 188. " Boys." A technical term for postilions.

Line 193. " Presented." Represented, took the part of, as commonly in Shakespeare.

Line 194. " Tide." Time, season.

Line 195. The " masque " was an allegorical occasional piece, generally designed for a special festival at the court or some other scene of importance, and produced with splendid circumstances of scenery, dresses, and music. The " pageant " was a gorgeous spectacular performance.

Lines 217–218. " Peal'd the nightingale," etc. Mrs. Anne Thackeray Ritchie says : " As Tennyson was walking at night in a friend's garden, he heard a nightingale singing with such a frenzy of passion that it was unconscious of everything else, and not frightened though he came and stood quite close beside it; he could see its eye flashing, and feel the air bubble in his ear through the vibration."

Line 219. "Pallas." The goddess of wisdom.

Line 220. "Blazon'd." Pictured; one with the constellations, representing the heavenly sphere; the other with the continents, representing the terrestrial globe.

Line 226. "Gave." Opened upon, gave access to.

Lines 232–234. The handwriting of women was formerly sloping or running, and hence the Prince's adoption of such script.

Line 238. "Cupid." The winged boy, god of love, always represented as blind.

Line 239. "Uranian Venus." The heavenly Venus, or spiritual love.

Line 244. "Glaz'd with muffled moonlight." Overlaid with the smooth radiance of the moon shining from behind a thin curtain of cloud.

Canto II. Line 1. Here the second speaker begins.

Line 8. "Sang." Murmured with the laurel's rustle.

Line 10. "Boss'd." Embossed, sculptured in relief; *i.e.* with the figures of the design standing out solidly from the surface.

Line 11. The "frieze" is that part of the outside of a classical building which is above the beam that rests on the tops of the pillars, and below the edge of the roof.

Line 13. "Muses and the Graces." The Muses, nine in number, — Clio, Euterpe, Thalia, Melpomene, Terpsichore, Erato, Polyhymnia, Urania, Calliope, — presided, each in her own province, over poetry, art, and science. They were of divine nature, and, with Apollo their leader, as the god of poetry, they stand for the higher activities of human life as their spiritual patrons. The Graces, three in number, — Euphrosyne, Aglaia, and Thalia, — were merely personifications of female beauty. The arrangement of these four groups round the fountain is designed to indicate the purpose of the college.

Line 38. "Your ideal," *i.e. you as his ideal*, not *his ideal, or idea, of you.*

Lines 40–41. "This barren . . . compliment." This vain profusion of wordiness, this false flattering tone that passes among men for courtesy.

Line 44. "The child." This rather humorously recalls her father's remark in Canto I., line 136.

Line 48. "Cast and fling." Cast off and fling away.

Line 49. "The tricks . . . of men." The little feminine weaknesses, as vanity, susceptibility to compliment, etc., of which men take advantage to enslave us.

Line 53. "Conscious of ourselves." Aware of our own identity, self-conscious, and consequently feeling embarrassed.

Line 54. "Perused the matting." Kept our eyes on the floor, as though examining the pattern of the carpet.

Line 60. "Enter'd on the boards." This is another Cambridge University technicality; there the register of undergraduates' names is officially known as "the boards."

Lines 62-71. "It is customary in English colleges," says Mr. Wallace, "to adorn the Hall or some other public room with portraits or statues of famous past members of the establishment. The college of the poem has no past, and the statues are those of eight of the most eminent women of antiquity, representing respectively legislative sagacity, political enterprise, military prowess, architectural skill, physical courage, intellectual culture, imperial ambition, and wifely devotion."

Line 63. "Odalisques." Beautiful female slaves of a Turkish harem.

Line 64. "Stunted squaws." Women unnaturally deformed in obedience to a perverse custom or erroneous conception of beauty, such as the Flatheads of the North American Indians. — "She." Egeria, a wood nymph, who gave laws to Numa Pompilius for the religious government of early Rome. He was "the Sabine" of line 65.

Line 65. "She." Semiramis, the famous legendary Assyrian queen, said to have built Babylon.

Line 67. "Artemisia." The queen who fought at Salamis on the side of Xerxes.

Line 68. "Rhodope." An English literary form of Rhodopis, an Egyptian woman celebrated for the act here mentioned, though it was wrongly ascribed to her.

Line 69. "Clelia." A Roman heroine, who escaped from Porsenna, to whom she had been given as a hostage, by swimming the Tiber on horseback. — "Cornelia." Daughter of the elder Scipio Africanus, and the mother of the Gracchi, the ideal of Roman motherhood.

Lines 69-70. "Palmyrene that fought Aurelian." Zenobia, the queen of Palmyra, who was captured by the Emperor Aurelian, and brought to Rome in triumph.

Line 71. "Agrippina." An ideal Roman matron of the empire,

granddaughter of Augustus, and wife of Germanicus, whom she accompanied on his campaigns in Germany.

Line 72.   "Convention."   Conventionality.

Line 73.   "Makes noble," etc.   Ennobles the mind through the senses.   Dawson compares Shelley, "Prince Athanase" : —

> "The mind becomes that which it contemplates;
>   And so Zonoras, by forever seeing
>   Their bright creations, grew like wisest men."

Line 94.   "Headed like a star."   With shining golden hair.

Line 95.   "A double April old," *i.e.* two years old.

Line 96.   "Aglaia."   A Greek word meaning *beauty, brightness.* It was the name of one of the Graces.

Lines 97–98.   "The dame that whisper'd."   The Phrygian king, Midas, told to his wife the secret of the changing of his ears to those of an ass.   She, unable to hold the secret, told it to the waters of a marsh, and the growing sedges whispered it to the world.

Lines 101–104.   These lines give a concise summary of the Nebular Hypothesis, as formulated by the French mathematician and astronomer, Laplace.   "It supposes the matter of the solar system to have existed originally in the form of a vast diffused revolving nebula, which, gradually cooling and consequently contracting towards the center, threw off, owing to the action of centrifugal force, successive rings of matter, from which subsequently by the same laws were produced the several planets, satellites, and other bodies of the system."

Line 104.   "Monster."   The vast animals of the early ages of the earth.

Line 105.   "Woaded."   Dyed with the blue of the woad plant, as the ancient Britons were.

Line 106.   "Raw from the prime."   Just come into being, and untouched by any refining influences — the primitive barbarian, fundamentally rude and brutal.

Line 110.   "Amazon."   A nation of female warriors of Asia Minor, celebrated in Greek legendary history.

Line 112.   "Appraised."   Praised, approved. — "The Lycian custom."   According to Herodotus, the Lycians differed from all other nations in taking their names from their mothers instead of their fathers, and in tracing their ancestry in the feminine rather than the masculine line.

Line 113.   "Lar and Lucumo."   Titles of honor borne respectively by the priests and the nobles among the ancient Etruscans. "Lay at wine with" seems to indicate the personal freedom and equality with men, enjoyed by the ladies of this nation.

Lines 114–116. "Ran down . . . from just." "In ancient Persia, and throughout Asia generally, women were for the most part regarded merely as a valuable property maintained for purposes of ostentation and voluptuousness, and to be jealously guarded as such. In the Homeric times of Greek history we find the wives and daughters of the Chiefs treated with marked deference and possessed of considerable influence, but with the progress of democratic institutions and the diffusion of a coarser spirit throughout society, their position became less honorable as their political importance diminished. After the Persian Wars, moreover, the Greeks appear to have become infected with Oriental ideas concerning the proper treatment of women; and in the fifth century, the period of their greatest power and development, they held much severer views on the subject than their forefathers of the Heroic Age. Their women were not indeed subjected to the insult of seclusion in harems under the custody of eunuchs, but they were restrained from social freedom as now understood in Europe, and the ideal held before them, at any rate in Athens, was a life of silent domesticity that should never attract the attention of the outside world, either for good or for evil. Consequently those Greek women whose names have come down to us as having won distinction in intellectual accomplishments were not ladies of good position, but such as had defied the ordinary social canons, and struck out a line for themselves. In Rome their condition was far otherwise. They were indeed excluded from political rights, and labored under certain civil disabilities in connection with property and other matters, but they were always treated with extreme personal attention and respect. The wife was the honored mistress of the house, and shared to the full in the reverence due to her husband. Women were not forbidden to appear in public, nor shut out from the advantages of education, and the history of the Roman Commonwealth contains the names of not a few ladies of culture and fine character who, without reproach, mingled in the life of their time, and devoted their talents and their energies to the national welfare" (Wallace).

Line 117. "Fulmined." A rare word, found in Milton. The common modern expression is "thundered." — "Laws Salique," *i.e.* laws forbidding inheritance to pass through a female line.

Line 118. "Little-footed China." Alluding to the custom practiced in China of cramping the feet of the girls in small shoes.

Lines 118–119. "Touch'd on Mahomet with much contempt." "The slurring over of the name, by allotting to its three syllables the space of one only, is no doubt designed by the poet to accentuate the fair lecturer's contempt for the prophet ; for a similar effect see IV. 309 below" (Wallace). Hallam Tennyson asks, "Does she allude to a report once popular that Mahomet denied that women have souls, or that, according to the Mohammedan doctrine, hell was chiefly peopled with women ? "

Line 119. "Chivalry." The system of military and social privileges which prevailed in Europe during the Middle Ages. By inculcating an ideal standard of action for men, — courtesy, generosity, valor, and honor, and a defense of the weak and the oppressed by the strong, — chivalry raised the estimate of women, as well as the manners of men.

Line 135. "If more was more." If a larger brain did really imply a more powerful intellect, if more in bulk was really more in power.

Line 143. "Horn-handed breakers of the glebe." Peasants, clod-breakers, plowmen, hard-handed laborers.

Line 144. "Verulam." Lord Bacon. Homer was eminent in poetry, Plato in philosophy, and Bacon in science.

Line 146. "Elizabeth." Queen Elizabeth of England.

Line 147. "Joan." Joan of Arc.

Line 148. "Sappho." A Greek poetess.

Line 149. "She." The Princess Ida.

Line 156. "Two heads in council." Man and woman.

Line 180. "Softer Adams." The women who were trying to be all that men are.

Line 180. "Academe." Academy: the name suggests, in this form, Plato's Academy, the source and pattern of the schools for higher instruction and learning in ancient days.

Line 181. "Sirens." Sea nymphs who, by their singing, fascinated sailors and drew them to shipwreck on the island rocks.

Line 188. "Weasel on a grange." It was formerly a custom to nail on the barn door any of the small wild creatures that commit petty depredations about a farm, as a warning to others of the species.

Line 205. "Who am not mine." Who cannot act in all things as I would, being subject to the Princess.

Line 224. "Bestrode." The characteristic posture as one stands over a fallen friend to defend him.

Line 227. "Branches." Ancestry and relationship are commonly referred to under the metaphor of trees and branches. "Current." Running lustily, vigorously.

Line 263. "Spartan Mother with emotion." Crush out, for the public good, all natural affection; a duty sternly inculcated among the ancient Spartans.

Line 264. "Lucius Junius Brutus." The establisher of the Roman Republic. He condemned his own sons to death for the public good.

Line 304. "Her mother's color." The color worn by those who were on her "side" of the College — the side of which she was tutor.

Line 316. "Elm and vine." Like the elm, and the vine that clings about it.

Line 319. "Danaïd." The Danaïds, daughters of Danaus, King of Argos, having murdered their husbands, were punished in Hades by condemnation to carry water in sieves. The expression therefore means "be found unable to keep your secret," "let it slip from you."

Line 320. "Ruin." The College and its purpose be ruined.

Line 323. "Aspasia." The most famous intellectual woman of Greece, the friend of Pericles, and the center of the group about him in Athens.

Line 325. "Sheba." The Queen of Sheba visited Solomon because of his wisdom. See 1 Kings x.

Line 420. "The second-sight . . . age." "According to the old legend, Astraea (Starbright), the daughter of Zeus and Themis (the goddess of justice), lived among men on earth during the Golden Age, and was the last of the Deities to leave when that had passed away. It was believed moreover that she would be the first to re-establish her home on earth should the Golden Age ever return. There is a famous reference to this theory in Virgil, and it reappears in many English poets — Milton, Pope, and notably in the title of Dryden's Ode in celebration of the Restoration of Charles II. in 1660, "Astraea Redux" (The Return of Astraea), by which the poet intended to indicate a joyful conviction that a new Age of Prosperity was dawning upon the country. "Second-sight" is the name given to the power of seeing future or distant events, which some people have been believed to possess. The expression in the text means therefore that the Princess's mind was all-engrossed in the prophetic vision of some glorious and ideal Era in the future" (Wallace).

Line 443. "The Fates." Three in number, Clotho, Lachesis, Atropos, represented as muffled because they hold the future in their breasts.

Canto III. Line 1. The third speaker begins here.

The two opening lines are highly beautiful. They remind one of Chaucer's most beautiful description of morning, lines 635–636 of the " Knight's Tale " : —

> " And firy Phebus riseth up so brighte
> That al the orient laugheth at the lighte."

Line 11. " The circled Iris." Denoting the circular, dark band round the eyes that tells of a long, sleepless night of tears.

Line 18. " Head." The principal or president of a college.

Line 24. " Canvass." Here means to criticise disparagingly and spitefully.

Line 34. " Rubric." Red, by her blushes, as certain letters or words are written in red, or *rubric*, in old manuscripts or books, and so stand out prominently and are easily read on the page.

Line 54. " Classic Angel." " Sweet girl graduate " who knows the classics.

Line 55. " Ganymedes." Ganymede was a beautiful Trojan youth, who was carried to heaven to be cupbearer to Zeus.

Line 56. " Vulcan " was cast from heaven and fell to the earth. See Pope's " Homer's Iliad," Book I., lines 760–765, and Milton's " Paradise Lost," Book I., lines 740–746.

Line 57. " This marble." He speaks thus of Lady Blanche, with reference to her inexorable determination. In like manner, " wax " denotes impressibility.

Line 58. " Furlough." Here means permission to remain.

Line 59. " Shook her doubtful curls." This expression means no more than " shook her head doubtfully " — to indicate her small hope of his success.

Line 73. " Inosculated." Blent together into one. The word is generally used in special derivative application to the case of veins and other vessels that have been made to run into one another, but here there is no doubt a closer reference to the etymology of the word, which is derived from the Latin *osculare*, " to kiss," and thus signifies primarily unity through affection.

Line 90. " Sphere." The highest, or the upper air.

Line 96. " Her, and her." Lady Psyche and Melissa.

Line 97. " Hebes." Hebe was the cupbearer to the gods before Ganymede.

Line 99. " Samian Herè." Wife of Zeus, whose favorite city was Samos.

Line 100. "Memnon." A name given to a colossal statue in Egypt, said to give forth a musical sound on being touched by the dawn's rays.

Line 109. "No fighting shadows here." A reference to the curse on the Royal House.

Line 110. "Crabb'd." Hard, impenetrable, like the shell of a crab. — "Gnarl'd." Full of gnars, or knots — used of timber that cannot be worked easily on that account.

Line 111. "Prime." Primeval. Here it means never touched by man since their creation.

Lines 111-112. Work at road making in the hottest season. The summer solstice occurs in the north about June 21.

Line 115. "At point to move." About to leave the room.

Line 120. "I fabled nothing fair." I invented no plausible story.

Line 126. "Limed." Ensnared, caught as a bird with birdlime, a sticky substance which, smeared on branches, holds fast birds that settle thereon.

Line 130. "Puddled." Made muddy, polluted.

Line 154. "The dip of certain strata." Measure their inclination to the horizon — go on a geological excursion for the purpose of making observations.

Line 158. "Ran up its furrowy forks." Shot up its two peaks.

Line 186. "The thing you say." Too harsh.

Line 194. "The bird of passage." The birds that leave the cold north in the autumn to spend the winter in the warmer south.

Line 212. "Vashti." Queen of Ahasuerus. See Esther i. 10-12.

Line 215. "Full East." Like an east wind.

Line 218. "Gray." Hoary, ancient.

Line 225. "Might I dread." May I dare to say.

Line 227. "Issue." Children.

Line 232. "Ourself the sacrifice." Devoted herself in self-sacrifice to her cause.

Line 233. "We are not talk'd to thus." Meaning that she is not accustomed to be addressed by her inferiors in this tone of familiar criticism.

Line 241. "Ourselves." The children are so much a part of the mother's life as to be her real self, the self through which she suffers more than in her single life.

Line 246. "πον στω." Archimedes said: "Give me *where I may stand*, and I'll move the earth."

Lines 250–254. Would that, instead of being short-lived like flies, we were able to live, like the giants, a thousand years, so that we might see our work, which requires a long age, slowly accomplished !

Line 254. "Sandy footprint." Footprints of birds and animals are sometimes found petrified.

Line 261. "Taboo." A Polynesian word denoting *restraint*, especially of a religious character. The speaker means that hitherto women, crushed down and confined by the tyranny of men, have been forbidden a chance of free development, mental or moral.

Line 262. "Dwarfs of the gynæceum" conveys exactly the same idea as the preceding line ; "dwarfs" refers to their stunted intellects and aspirations.

Lines 266–268. These three lines may perhaps be rendered plainer by an inversion: "If our aim were more easily to be achieved by some single act of self-sacrifice or any form of death than by slow methods."

Lines 269–270. "Against the pikes . . . down the fiery gulf." These two expressions, according to Mr. Wallace's conjecture, were not used vaguely : "They were probably suggested by two legends of ancient Rome: (1) In the Latin War (B.C. 340) Publius Decius Mus, one of the Roman generals, sacrificed himself on the spears of the enemy in order to secure the victory to his army, it having been revealed to him in a vision from Heaven that one army was doomed, and the general of the other. (A somewhat similar act of devotion is recorded of Arnold von Winkelried in the battle of Sempach, 1388, during the Swiss struggle for independence against the Austrians ; this hero, seeing that the Austrian line of spears was impregnable, gathered into his breast as many as he could, and falling upon them created a gap into which his comrades poured). (2) A chasm having appeared in the market place of Rome, and the priests having declared that this would not close up until there had been cast into it the chief element of Rome's greatness, a young noble named Marcus Curtius, thinking that this condition would best be fulfilled by the sacrifice of one of her sons, leapt into it on horseback and in full armor (B.C. 362)."

Line 280. "Dare we dream." Dare we suppose that the God who made us is like a workman who improves by practice ?

Line 285. "Diotima." A wise woman of Mantinea, whom Socrates, in Plato's "Symposium," calls his instructress.

Line 292. "We shudder but to dream." Referring to vivisection, and the assertion that dogs have sometimes been fed with the fragments of the dissecting-room.   Dawson quotes " The Children's Hospital " : —

" I could think he was one of those who would break their jests on
     the dead,
   And mangle the living dog that had loved him and fawned at his
     knee —
   Drenched with the hellish oorali — that ever such things should be ! "

He adds : " In one of Hogarth's series of *The Four Stages of Cruelty*
is a print which, may have suggested this passage.   It represents a
dissecting-table at Surgeons' Hall, upon which a subject is stretched
out, and dogs are eating the intestines, which are falling upon the
floor."

Line 298.   " Encarnalize."   Make carnal, sensualize.

Line 299.   " Hangs."   Undecided.

Lines 306–313.   " She becomes really profound," says Dawson, " in
her analysis of our notions of creation as stages of successive acts.
Our minds, she teaches, are so constituted that we must *of necessity*
apprehend everything in the form and aspect of successive time ; but
in the Almighty fiat, ' Let there be light,' the whole of the complex
potentialities of the universe were in fact hidden."

Line 324.   " Elysian lawns."   Elysium was the abode of the blessed
after death, sometimes placed in the Islands of the Blest, to which
Tennyson himself refers this passage.   The " Demigods " are the
heroes of antiquity.

Line 331.   " Corinna's triumph."   Corinna, the Greek poetess, over-
came Pindar, the most famous Greek writer of odes, several times in
the trial for the prize of poetry at the public games.

Line 334.   " Victor."   Pindar.

Lines 344–345.   These names are of rocks of various natures and
structures, and are used here in amused and playful irony.

Song.   " This song, it is supposed, was inspired by the bugle music
of the boatmen at Lake Killarney.   The first peal of the notes is loud
and triumphant.   The poet's mind is carried back by the martial sound
and the distant sight of the ruined walls of Killarney Castle to the
far dim mediæval past.   The impression is intense, but fades quickly
as the warlike strain dies away.   The echoes now suggest the silver
tinkle of elfin horns, and for a moment the eerie charm of fairyland
holds the listener.   These too die, and with the silence comes the swift
lyric turn from the visions of exhausted feudalism and of fruitless

superstition to the clear, certain life of the present and of the future. That life is to bring the gradual union of his nature with that of his beloved; to be full of the gentle enduring influences which, like echoes, 'roll from soul to soul,' but, unlike echoes, 'grow forever and forever'" (Boynton).

Canto IV. Line 1. The fourth speaker begins here.

Line 2. "Hypothesis." The Nebular Hypothesis.

Line 5. "Coppice-feather'd." Lightly fringed with foliage.

Line 21. "Tears, idle tears." "The idea of this lyric had been resting in the poet's mind since 1831. Then at the age of twenty-two he published in *The Gem*, one of the annuals at that time in fashion, the following poem, omitted from all the recent editions of his works:—

> " 'O sad *No more!*   O sweet *No more!*
>   O strange *No more!*
>   By a mossed brookbank on a stone
>   I smelt a wildwood flower alone ;
>   There was a ringing in my ears,
>   And both my eyes gushed out with tears,
>   Surely all pleasant things had gone before,
>   Low-buried fathom-deep beneath with thee,
>   *No more!* '

The melancholy melody of the refrain ' No more ' has evidently haunted the poet's mind, and he has taken the poem which he justly suppressed as unworthy of him, and after long years reproduced it in this glorified form. There is nothing like it in English, save Keats's ' Ode to a Nightingale.' In that poem the word ' forlorn ' has evidently charmed the ear of the poet in the same manner " (Dawson).

Mr. George Grove, in an interesting "commentary" on this song (*Macmillan's Magazine,* November, 1866), says : "The keynote is clearly and beautifully struck in the first stanza. Nothing moves the spirit of man so profoundly as some of the appearances of nature ; more profoundly because it is often impossible to explain why it should be so. The vague but intense yearning, the feeling of vastness and longing, which possesses one at the sight of certain aspects of the sunset, has been felt by almost every one. . . . The same kind of feeling, only more personal and less vast, and colored rather by wild, passionate human regret, is apt to seize the mind in autumn, in viewing some scene of sweet, rich, peaceful beauty, like the ' happy autumn fields ' of this poem. . . . The keynote of ' some divine despair ' in the heart is

touched. Persons and incidents, fraught with unutterable recollec-
tions, and worth all the world to one, — a dead child, a lost love, a
sudden look, a parting, a difference, a reconciliation, — present them-
selves with peculiar power. It is perhaps long since we had to do with
them, but they come back as 'fresh' as if it were yesterday; they fill
the mind as if present, in all their sweetness and familiar tender dear-
ness, and the pang of absence, and the maddening sense of the utter
irrecoverableness of the past, rushes in after them with a 'wild regret,'
and the tears, the 'idle tears' — not idle in themselves, but idle only
because 'we know not what they mean' — 'rise from the depths' of
our 'divine despair,' — divine because so utterly beyond all human
reason or knowledge, — and gather, smarting, in the eyes of the
gazer."

Line 27. "The underworld." Here means that part of the world
below the horizon, and from which a ship seems to come up from the
deep into sight.

Line 47. "Cram our ears with wool." The allusion is to the hero
of the "Odyssey," who stopped the ears of his comrades with wax
that they might not be enchanted with the singing of the Sirens.

Line 59. "Cancel'd Babels." Completely destroyed Babylons;
here used metaphorically of all the dead past. — "Kex." "Hem-
lock; let the rough growth of the ruin break through the starry
mosaic pavement, and the goat, with his beard blowing in the wind,
hang on the pillar (as on a crag), and the wild fig tree split the mon-
strous idols of the shrine (just as the pine splits the rock in whose
crevices it has sprung up). These picturesque details of the ruin of a
temple are the characteristic ones noticed by travelers, and are famil-
iar in literature, both ancient and modern" (Woodberry).

Line 69. "A death's-head at the wine." According to the Egyp-
tian custom mentioned by Herodotus: "At their convivial banquets,
among the wealthy classes, when they have finished supper, a man
carries round in a coffin the image of a dead body carved in wood,
made as like as possible in color and workmanship, and in size gener-
ally about one or two cubits in length; and showing this to each of
the company, he says, 'Look upon this, then drink and enjoy your-
self; for when dead you will be like this.'"

Line 100. "Like the Ithacensian suitors." Mr. Dawson says:
"The suitors at the court of Penelope feel the occult influence of the
unseen goddess Pallas causing their thoughts to wander. They fail
to recognize Ulysses in his disguise, and their laughter is constrained
and unnatural, they know not why. They 'laugh with alien lips,'

which is the nearest possible poetical translation of the Greek idiomatic expression, 'They laughed with other men's jaws.' "

Line 104. " Bulbul." Nightingale. — "Gulistan." Rose-garden. Both words are Persian.

Line 110. " When we made bricks in Egypt." When we lived in bondage to men, before the exodus to this retreat. The phrase is a general one for thraldom, and alludes to the work required by Pharaoh of the Israelites in Egypt. See the first and fifth chapters of Exodus.

Line 121. " Valkyrian hymns." Such as were sung by the Valkyrs, or Valkyrias, "the choosers of the slain," or fatal sisters of Odin in the Northern mythology. They were represented as awful and beautiful maidens, who, mounted on swift horses and bearing drawn swords, presided over the field of battle, selecting those destined to death, and conducting them to Valhalla, where they ministered at the feasts of the heroes.

Line 126. " Hymen." In Greek mythology, the god of marriage.

Line 130. " Owed to none." Bound to none, responsible to none.

Line 137. " With whom the bell-mouth'd glass had wrought." On whom the wine had taken effect.

Line 160. " Glow to gloom." From the light within the tent to the darkness without.

Line 166. "The weight . . . world." " Mark the exquisite irony of this line. As though his struggle in the water was rendered the harder by the fact that on the lady rested the fate of this great movement ! This is the true touch of ironical banter. There is a similar passage in the Roman poet Statius, where the baby Apollo is represented as depressing by his divine weight the edge of the island of Delos as he crawls along it " (Wallace).

Line 180. " Indian craft." Woodcraft.

Line 183. " Caryatids." In Greek architecture, female figures used as pillars of support.

Line 184. " A weight of emblem." The allegorical adornment between the cornice and the architrave. — " Valves." The gates.

Line 185. " The hunter." Actæon, who was changed into a stag by Diana, because of his intrusion upon her while bathing. He is here represented in the openwork of the gates, with the form and face of a man, but the antlers have sprouted on his brows, and, branching above, make the spikes of the gate.

Line 194. " Bear." The northern constellation of Ursa Major. It is composed of seven stars near and about the North Star.

Line 207. "Judith." The Jewess who entered the camp of Holo-
fernes, then besieging her native city, and, gaining admission to his
tent under pretext, killed him as he lay asleep after the feast, and cut
off his head. Florian hid himself behind a statue which represented
Judith holding the head of the slain Holofernes in her hand. For the
story of Judith and Holofernes, see the Book of Judith in the Apocrypha.

Line 217. "Either guilt." The guilt of both.

Line 227. "Proper to the clown." Characteristic of the vulgar and
ill-bred, whether clad in laborer's homespun or royal purple.

Line 242. "Thrid." Thread. — "Musky-circled." Hung with
heavy fragrance.

Line 243. "Boles." Tree trunks.

Line 250. "Mnemosyne." Goddess of memory, mother of the
Muses.

Line 252. "Haled." Hauled.

Line 255. "Mystic fire." St. Elmo's fire, called *corposant* by sail-
ors, is an electrical ball of light that sometimes plays about the masts
and rigging of a ship in or before stormy weather.

Line 260. "Blowzed." Ruddy. Kennett says: "A girl or wench
whose face looks red by running abroad in the wind and weather, is
called a *blouz*, and said to have a blouzing color."

Line 261. "A Druid rock." The reference is to the strong pillars
of stone, such as those at Stonehenge, considered to be the relics of
the Druid worship.

Line 263. "Wail'd about with mews." Surrounded by crying
sea mews or gulls.

Line 275. "Castalies." Castalia was the fountain on Mount Par-
nassus, sacred to the Muses, and inspiring to poetry those who drank
of it.

Line 292. "Jonah's gourd." The story of the gourd may be found
in the fourth chapter of the Book of Jonah.

Line 306. "Lidless." Vigilant, as never closing the eyes.

Lines 307–308. "My foot was to you." I was about to go to you.

Line 310. "You had gone." You would have gone, she would
have told, etc.

Line 313. "Nursery." Meaning a nursery garden, a place for
growing young trees.

Line 339. "Wisp." Will-o'-the-wisp, seen in marshes and low
lands.

Lines 346–347. "I built the nest . . . to hatch the cuckoo." The
reference here is to the fact that the cuckoo does not build a nest for

itself, but deposits its eggs in that of some other bird, the sparrow for preference, to whom also it leaves the task of rearing the young bird. The speaker means that she has undergone all the labor connected with the establishment of the institution, and now her rival is to enter into the enjoyment of its results.

Line 352. "A Niobëan daughter." Queen Niobe of Thebes, according to Greek legend, had twelve children, and boasted over Latona, who had but two. Thereupon these two, Apollo and Artemis, cast arrows from heaven and slew each of the twelve. Niobe herself was changed by Zeus into stone, and ever continued to weep for her sad fate.

Line 366. "When the wild peasant." Referring to the incendiary fires so common in the troubles with the English agricultural laborers some years before the poem was written. In his "To Mary Boyle," Tennyson himself reports a personal experience in one of these : —

> "And once — I well remember that red night
> When thirty ricks,
> All flaming, made an English homestead Hell —
> These hands of mine
> Have helped to pass a bucket from the well
> Along the line."

Line 401. "The child of regal compact." The offspring of the sacred vow of the two kings. A compact between kings is more sacred than one between other men, because of the divine authority with which they rule — was the old faith.

Line 418. "Sphered up with Cassiopëia." Up among the stars, like the Ethiopian queen Cassiopëia, who became the constellation that bears her name ; or down in Hades, like Persephone (or Proserpina), whom Pluto carried off from earth and made his queen.

Line 420. "Winters of abeyance." The years during which the "pre-contract" lay in abeyance ; existed, but was not acted on.

Line 422. "Frequence." Throng.

Line 426. "Landskip." Landscape.

Line 427. "Dwarfs of presage." They turned out, when seen, to be less than was promised or expected.

Line 436. "The seal does music." The fact is stated by many naturalists. See "Encyclopædia Britannica," under *Seal*.

Line 466. "Babel." The reference is to the "Confusion of Tongues."

Line 472.   "Fixt like a beacon tower."   As Dawson notes, the same simile occurs in "Enoch Arden":—

> "Allured him as the beacon blaze allures
>   The bird of passage, till he madly strikes
>   Against it, and beats out his weary life."

See also Longfellow's "The Lighthouse," published two years after "The Princess":—

> "The sea bird wheeling round it, with the din
>   Of wings and winds and solitary cries,
> Blinded and maddened by the light within,
>   Dashes himself against the glare, and dies."

Line 480.   "Those."   Her brothers.

Line 484.   "Protomartyr."   First martyr, the name given to St. Stephen.

Line 494.   "Chattels."   Articles of personal property.   Wallace quotes the Slavonian definition of woman as "a living broom or shovel."

Line 495.   "Turnspits."   Mere cooks, servants set to turn the spit, or pointed rod, on which it was the custom to fix meat to be roasted by turning it from side to side before the open fire.

Line 552.   "Norway sun."   Upon the Arctic circle the sun does not set on midsummer day, June 22, but remains above the horizon for twenty-four hours.   Norway stands for the Northern country, because it is along its shores that travelers commonly coast to witness the midnight sun.   At that time and place the sun does not set, but remains constantly in the heavens night and day.   The Prince means that the light of his love was thus constant.

Canto V.   Line 1.   Here the fifth speaker begins.

Line 2.   "Stationary voice."   The voice of a sentinel.

Line 4.   "The second two."   Cyril and Psyche were the first two; the Prince and Florian the second.

Line 5.   "His Highness."   The King, the Prince's father.

Line 6.   "Lanes and walls of canvas."   The lines of tents of the King's army.

Line 9.   "Blazon'd lions."   Lions pictured (emblazoned) on the ensign.

Line 13.   "Innumerous."   Innumerable.

Line 15. "A strangled titter." They attempt to strangle their irreverent laughter at the Prince.

Line 16. "Clamoring etiquette to death." Killing or disregarding etiquette. Ordinarily, good manners would restrain the nobles and officers from noticing openly the Prince's ridiculous plight, but on this occasion the ludicrous spectacle was too much for them, and after a slight attempt at the preservation of their gravity they burst out unrestrainedly.

Line 21. "Gilded Squire." Gorgeously dressed squire.

Line 25. "Mawkin." A mere servant girl.

Line 30. "Beneath his vaulted palm." Hollowing his hand over his mouth.

Line 37. "Transient." Passing, making the transition.

Line 38. "Woman-slough." Woman garments. "Slough" refers to the skin thrown off by the snake at his periodical renovation.

Line 40. "Harness." Armor.

Line 45. "Resolder'd peace." Repaired peace; peace made whole again.

Line 110. "At parle." In parley, in conference.

Line 121. "Trampled year." Trampled harvest.

Line 125. "Lightens scorn." Flashes scorn, as lightning, from her eyes.

Line 132. "Shards." Fragments, used of hard, earthen substances. — "Catapults." Engines for bombardment.

Line 136. "Flitting chance." Passing chance, with a suggested meaning of slight hope.

Line 141. "With ribs of wreck." Like a wrecked ship, the ribs of which remain long after the lighter parts are fallen away.

Line 142. "Mammoth." The huge elephant of former geologic age, still found embedded ("bulk'd") in the ice banks of Siberia.

Line 146. "That idiot legend." The legend of the Sorcerer. Canto I., line 5 : —

"There lived an ancient legend in our house."

Line 157. "Dash'd with death." Bespattered with blood.

Line 162. "A cherry net." A net to protect cherries from the birds.

Line 170. "Gagelike." As the knight flung his glove, or gage of battle, before his enemy as a sign of challenge to combat.

Line 179. "Satyr." A mythological being, half human and half goatish by nature ; here used as a metaphor for the vile and coarse.

Line 183.   "Magnetic."   Turning toward and becoming charged with.

Line 190.   "Piebald."   Spotted with different colors.

Line 195.   "Mooted."   Put in question, disputed, debated.

Line 227.   "Huge trees, a thousand rings."   Trees a thousand years old, the growth of each year making one ring in the trunk.

Line 229.   "Valentines."   Love-messages.

Line 250.   "The airy Giant's zone."   The belt of Orion.

Line 252.   "Alters hue," etc.   Dawson quotes Proctor's "Myths and Marvels of Astronomy " : " Every bright star when close to the horizon shows these colors, and so much the more distinctly as the star is the brighter.   Sirius, which surpasses the brightest stars of the northern hemisphere full four times in luster, shows these changes of color so conspicuously that they were regarded as specially characteristic of this star, insomuch that Homer speaks of Sirius (not by name, but as the ' Star of Autumn ') shining most beautifully ' when laved of ocean's wave,' — that is, when close to the horizon."

Dawson adds : "The expression 'laved of ocean's wave' explains the 'washed with morning' of our poet.   The glitter of the early morning sun on the bright helmets of the brothers, and the glance of light upon the armor as they rode, are vividly realized in this beautiful simile.

"The passage of Homer referred to is 'Iliad,' V. 5, and is thus rendered by Merivale : —

" ' Flashed from his helm and buckler a bright incessant gleam,
    Like summer star that burns afar, new bathed in ocean's stream.'

And by Lord Derby : —

" ' Forth from his helm and shield a fiery light
      There flashed, like autumn's star, that brightest shines
      When newly risen from his ocean bath.'

" The rendering *summer* star is beyond question the more correct. It is the star which is in the ascendant at the *time of ripening*, that is, during the *dog-days*."

Line 254.   "Morions."   Helmets.

Line 266.   "'S death !"   Contracted from the old oath "God's death," meaning the death on the Cross.

Line 283.   "St. something."   The reference is to St. Catharine of Alexandria, round whose name has grown up a vast amount of legendary lore. She is said to have lived about the beginning of the fourth century, and to have been the daughter of Costus, the half-brother of Constantine, by Sabinella, Queen of Egypt, whom she succeeded on the throne of that country. She was remarkable for her learning and culture, which have won for her the title of Patron Saint of Philosophy, and especially of ladies of high birth who pursue this study. According to the commonly received legend, the Emperor Maxentius sent the fifty wisest men of his court to convert her from Christianity, but she confuted them all with their own weapons of scholarly rhetoric, and won them over to her faith.

Line 319. "False daughters." The ducklings she has hatched.

Line 337. "An island-crag." "I have been out for a walk with A. T.," wrote Arthur Hugh Clough in September, 1861, "to a sort of island between two waterfalls, with pines on it, of which he retained a recollection from his visit of thirty-one years ago, and which, moreover, furnished a simile to 'The Princess.' He is very fond of this place, evidently."

Line 355. "Tomyris." The queen of the Massagetæ, who, after defeating and killing Cyrus, took his head, and dipping it in blood, bade him drink his fill. She had sworn that if he fought against her he should have all the blood he desired.

Lines 367–370. "Of lands," etc. "Allusion is made in the first two lines to Russian customs in the seventeenth century. One was that the bride, on her wedding day, should present her husband, in token of submission, with a whip made by her own hands. Another was, that on arriving at the nuptial chamber the bridegroom ordered the bride to pull off his boots. In the one was a whip, in the other a trinket. If she pulled off the one with the whip first, the groom gave her a slight blow. It is worthy of note that, according to Bracton, a wife is *sub virga*, under the rod, and Blackstone says that moderate correction with a stick is lawful.

"The last two lines refer to the Hindoo *Suttee*, now abolished, in conformity with which widows were burned upon the funeral pyres of their husbands" (Dawson).

Lines 367–373. The presentation by the bride of a whip to her future husband is an old Russian custom. The allusions which follow are to the Hindoo customs of burning widows on the funeral pyre of their husbands, and of casting female children into the Ganges.

Line 382. "Institutes." Laws, regulations.

Line 404. "Gadfly." This present petty trouble.

Line 408. "Yoked with children's." She means that hitherto

women and children have been classed together; that women have been regarded as having no more rights than children.

Line 412. "All that orbs." The whole orb of the earth, from pole to pole.

Line 417. "Arms fail'd." Psyche and Blanche. — "Egypt-plague." The reference is to the plagues visited upon the Egyptians because of the cruelty shown by Pharaoh towards the Israelites.

Line 423. "Authentic mother." She wishes to regard the one who forms the child's mind as its authentic mother.

Line 434. "When the man wants weight." Mr. Dawson quotes an interesting scientific enunciation of this theory from Dr. Antoinette Brown Blackwell's "The Sexes throughout Nature," from which (pages 96–97) I transcribe one sentence: "Whenever brilliantly colored male birds have acquired something of maternal habits, tastes, and impulses, conversely the female seem always to have acquired some counterbalancing weight of male characters. They are large in relative size, are brilliantly colored, are active and quarrelsome, or are a little of all these together. The large majority of birds illustrate this law."

Line 441. "The gray mare." The allusion is to the proverb, "The gray mare is the better horse," used of a wife who rules her husband. Rev. Lyman Abbott says : —

"The normal and divine order is the order in which the husband is the head of the household. Do not misunderstand me. I am not affirming that man is superior to woman. It has been often affirmed, and I repudiate it with indignation. There is no question of superiority or inferiority. The question is of headship, not of superiority. It is man who is to do the work and take the responsibilities, in order that woman may minister to love and life. That is the reason I do not believe in woman's suffrage. . . . Man should be the defender, and man should be the burden-bearer. I cannot altogether look with enthusiasm upon the new era in which women are rushing into every kind of employment, and lowering the wages of men by doing men's work. I would not close the door against them, nor shut them out from any vocation ; I would give them the largest liberty, all the liberty I claim for myself ; but, fellow-men, you and I, with our strong arms, ought to fight life's battles, and win life's bread, and leave the women free from the burden of bread-winning and battling, that they may minister to the higher life of faith, hope, and love."

The late Professor John Stuart Blackie, of the University of Edinburgh, wrote : —

"In the main it always was, and always must be, true, that even in the administration of the family affairs the man is the head of the woman ; let her be content to have the heart, which is the soul, and the hands which work the grace of domestic economy ; but outside this sphere, in the clamorous atmosphere of public life, or the platform of political wrangling or ecclesiastical thunder, the seldomer she appears the better."

Line 488. "Two bulks." Arac's brothers.

Line 491. "Mellay." Mêlée, a combat, a tourney.

Line 500. "Miriam and a Jael." Miriam, the Hebrew prophetess, who sang to the cymbals the song of triumph over Pharaoh by the Red Sea. See the fifteenth chapter of Exodus. Jael, the Jewish woman who killed Sisera by driving a nail through his temple. See the fourth chapter of Judges.

Line 503. "Saint's glory." The ring of light round the head of a saint as represented in pictures — the halo.

Canto VI. Line 1. The sixth speaker begins here.

Line 16. "Dame of Lapidoth." Deborah, wife of Lapidoth, who sang the song of triumph over Sisera — one of the grandest war songs in literature. See the fourth and fifth chapters of Judges.

Line 25. "The red cross." Signifying that the tree is to be cut down.

Lines 46–47. "A day blanch'd in our annals." This means to mark the day as a future holiday, a white day.

Line 49. "Spring." Blossoms.

Line 65. "Isles of light." By the expression "the tremulous isles of light," the Poet meant, as he has explained in a letter to Mr. Dawson, "spots of sunshine coming through the leaves, and seeming to slide from one to the other, as the procession of girls ' moves under *shade*.' "

Line 70. "Fretwork." His antlers.

Line 94. "The painting and the tress." See Canto I., lines 37–38.

Lines 109–111. "If so . . . the woman's goal." "This refers to her own sense of deep obligation to the Prince, to whom she owes no less than her life, and to her brothers, who have fought and won for her ; the recognition thus forced upon her, of the more general constant dependence of her sex upon the superior strength of the other, causes her to feel somewhat less confident than hitherto of the eventual success of her policy of isolation, and her claim to equality in all points with men " (Wallace).

Line 118. "Golden brede." Embroidered with gold.

Line 158. "Nemesis" was to the Greeks the goddess of moral jus-
tice, and as such was most commonly regarded as the personification
of Divine Retribution for insolence or reckless defiance of established
principles.

Lines 178–179. "Made no purple in the distance." Gave me no
bright, happy, future prospect.

Line 186. "In the dead prime." In the darkness just before day-
light.

Lines 205–206. "The woman is so hard upon the woman." Dawson
says : "This unamiable trait results from woman's mission as the con-
servator of society. In this respect, woman's character is very nar-
row, but she feels instinctively that she cannot afford to be lax in
offenses against social laws. Psyche's weakness had in fact broken up
Ida's university, and sins against the family tend to break up society."

In "The Scarlet Letter" Hawthorne gives us the conversation of a
group of women who are discussing the sentence imposed by men upon
Hester Prynne. "Goodwives," said a hard-featured dame of fifty,
"I'll tell you a piece of my mind. It would be greatly for the public
behoof if we women, being of mature age and churchmembers in good
repute, should have the handling of such malefactors as this Hester
Prynne. If the hussy stood up for judgment before us five that are
now here in a knot together, would she come off with such a sentence
as the worshipful magistrates have awarded ? Marry, I trow not!"

Line 224. "Stiff as Lot's wife." She was turned into a pillar of
salt as a punishment for disobedience. The story is told in the nine-
teenth chapter of Genesis.

Line 239. "Sine and arc," etc. Terms of the higher mathematics
and astronomy.

Line 283. "Adit." Entrance, access.

Line 298. "Song." See Canto IV., line 21.

Line 310. "Wintry." Cruel, pitiless.

Line 319. "The Pharos." This was a famous lighthouse built on
the island of Pharos, near Alexandria, by Ptolemy Philadelphus.

Line 338. In heraldry the "supporters" are the figures which
flank the central shield of a coat of arms ; as, for example, in the arms
of Great Britain.

Line 348. "Moon." Diana is represented with her symbol, the
crescent moon, above her head like a crown.

Line 352. "Ordinance." Orders.

Line 355. "Due." The due of, that which illness should have.

Canto VII. Line 1. Here the seventh and last speaker begins.

Line 18. "Leaguer." The armies lying as in siege about the place.

Line 19. "Void was her use." Gone was her customary occupation.

Line 23. "Verge." Horizon.

Line 25. "Tarn." A small dark lake or pond.

Line 31. "Gyres." Circles. Wallace makes the following note : "This line affords a good instance both of the Poet's minute observation of nature, and of his power of condensing his full meaning within the compass of very few words. The striking characteristics of the lark are, firstly, the clear sparkling melody of his notes, and, secondly, the strong impulse that dominates him to hurl himself aloft while singing, his upward flight being however a peculiar continuous fluttering ascent, which takes a spiral course, widening as the bird rises higher and higher into the air. Thus every word in the line is eminently appropriate. The lark was no doubt selected for mention in this passage owing to the pathetic contrast which its blithe and jubilant freedom offers to the mournful confinement and languor of the Prince."

Line 45. "Silks." The silk hangings or draperies of the bed.

Line 60. "Built." Built his hopes.

Line 88. "Dead." The dead of night.

Line 109. "The Oppian law." "This was a sumptuary law passed during the time of the direst distress of Rome, when Hannibal was almost at the gates. It enacted that no woman should wear a gay-colored dress, or have more than a half an ounce of gold ornaments, and that none should approach within a mile of any city or town in a car drawn by horses. The war being concluded, and the emergency over, the women demanded the repeal of the law. They gained one consul, but Cato, the other one, resisted. The women rose, thronged the streets and forum, and harassed the magistrates until the law was repealed" (Dawson).

Line 112. "The tax." "A heavy tax imposed on Roman matrons by the second triumvirate. No man was found bold enough to oppose it ; but Hortensia, daughter of Hortensius, the celebrated orator, spoke so eloquently against it, that her oration was preserved to receive the praise of Quintilian. She was successful" (Dawson).

Line 113. "Ax and eagle." The ax signifying civil power in the Roman Republic, and the eagle military.

Line 115. "Wolf's milk." Referring to the old familiar fable or legend that Romulus and Remus, the founders of Rome, when exposed to hunger and death in infancy, were suckled by a she-wolf.

Line 148. "That other." "Aphrodite (Venus) rising from the sea. Bayard Taylor calls the passage 'an exquisite rapid picture of Aphrodite floating along the wave to her home at Paphos; but,' he adds, 'what must we think of the lover, who, in relating the supreme moment of his passion, could turn aside to interpolate it? Its very loveliness emphasizes his utter forgetfulness of the governing theme.' It seems to us natural enough in the 'relating,' especially as it leads up to the impassioned

> 'nor end of mine,
> Stateliest for thee!' —

which shows that he has dwelt upon the picture of the goddess because he half identifies her with Ida" (Rolfe).

Line 167. "Danaë to the stars." Wholly open to their influence. Danaë was an Argive Princess, who was confined in an inaccessible tower of safety, but Zeus obtained admittance to her in the form of a shower of gold. Notice the appropriateness of the expression when used of the exposure of the earth to the influence of the golden stars.

Line 189. "Silver horns." The imagery of the song is of Swiss scenery, and the silver horns (as Matterhorn) are white mountain tops.

Line 191. "The firths of ice." Glaciers which pile up ("huddle") ice in their downward passage, break in crevasses ("furrow-cloven"), and melt when they reach the lower and warmer parts of the mountain. The "dusky" discharge is dark by comparison with the ice and snow from which it issues.

Line 198. "Water-smoke." The narrow cascades, which separate into drops through the great height of the fall, and appear like smoke. Tennyson observed them on his Pyrenean journey, from which, as he himself says, much of his mountain scenery is derived.

Line 201. "Pillars of the hearth." The columns of smoke rising from the chimneys.

Line 230. "Signs." The twelve signs of the Zodiac, through which lies the sun's apparent path in the heaven of stars.

Line 245. "Out of Lethe." Here simply means out of oblivion, from the moment of birth.

Line 255. "Burgeon." Blossom.

Lines 271–279 may be paraphrased thus: "'And so these two, the man and the woman, in some distant age, when the fullness of time has come, shall sit throned together, in perfect development of soul and body, sowing the seed that shall ripen to the harvest of the future, each inspired with a strong reverence both for self and for the other, each distinct from the other in the special characteristics of sex, but both enjoying the perfect unity that springs from perfect love. Then shall come back Paradise among men in all its primeval purity and splendor, then shall enter in the era of ideal marriage, free from all brute passion ; then shall humanity achieve its highest consummation.' A belief in the final perfectibility of the human race pervades the work of Tennyson " (Wallace).

Line 308. "Music." The metaphor is derived from the poetical belief that the stars make music in their motions.

Line 321. "Thee woman." That thou wast woman.

Lines 339–345. "My wife, my life ! Oh, we will walk this world." A striking contrast to this scene of "The Princess" is that in "Guinevere,"—

"Lo ! I forgive thee, as Eternal God forgives."

"When we shall have applied to all the problems of society the new and as yet unused elements which exist in womanhood, all results will be reached twice as quickly as they are now reached, all human work will be twice as quickly done, and then, perhaps, some new poet will write a new 'Princess'" (Stopford Brooke).